FINAL TOUCH OUTDOORS.

The Art of Coloring

This book is full of great things to color. Coloring re-laxes and helps with stress and

Anxiety. Landscapes are easy to color and be creative. A Great Pass time.

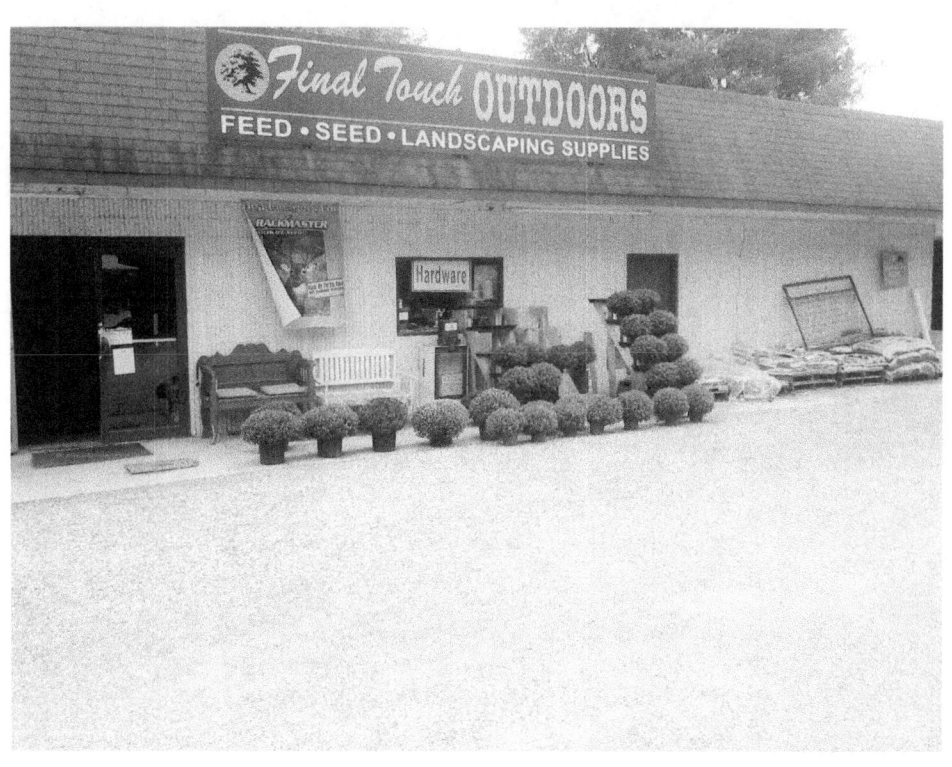

Final Touch a **GREAT** place to buy farm and garden supplies. They have a good stock of pet supplies, seeds, pet and farm animal food, meds and much, much more. And the *Boss* is humorous. He can make you laugh.

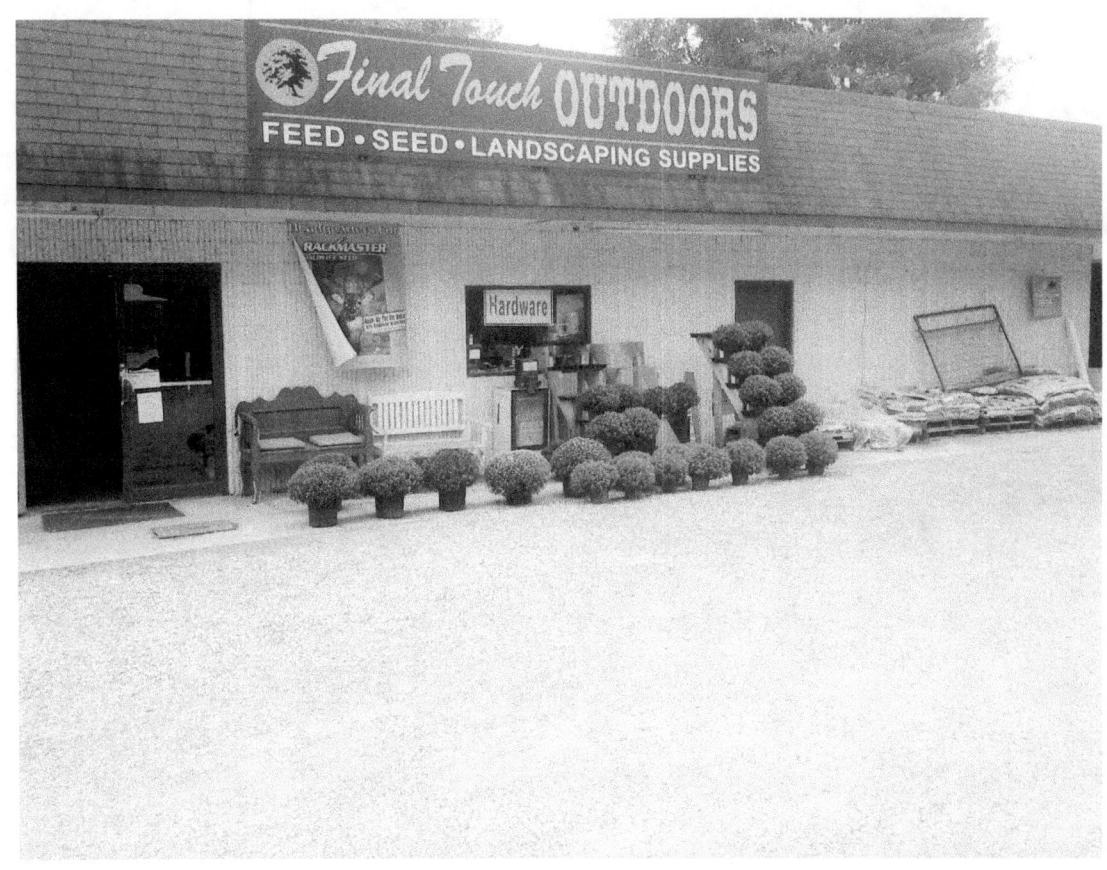

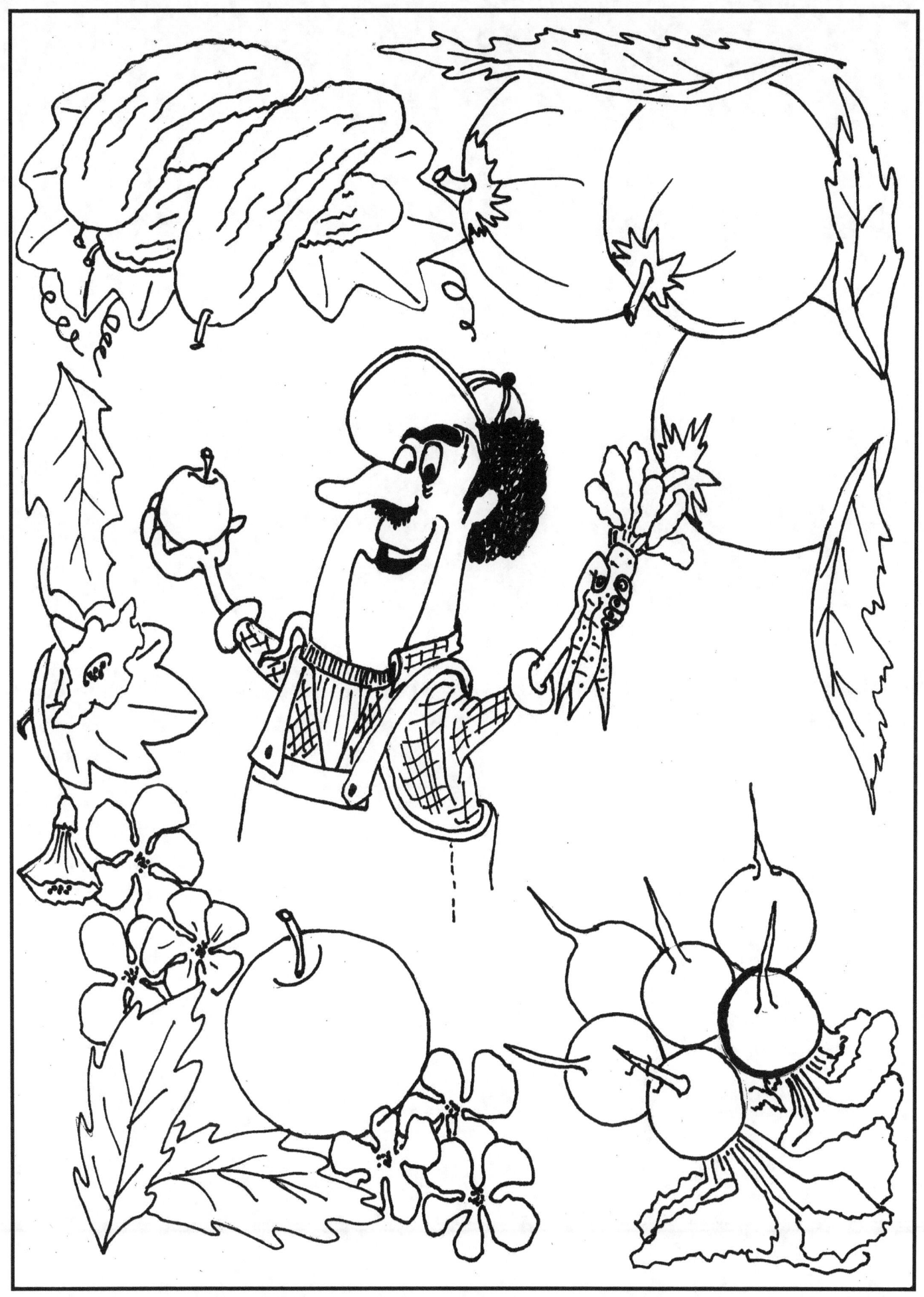

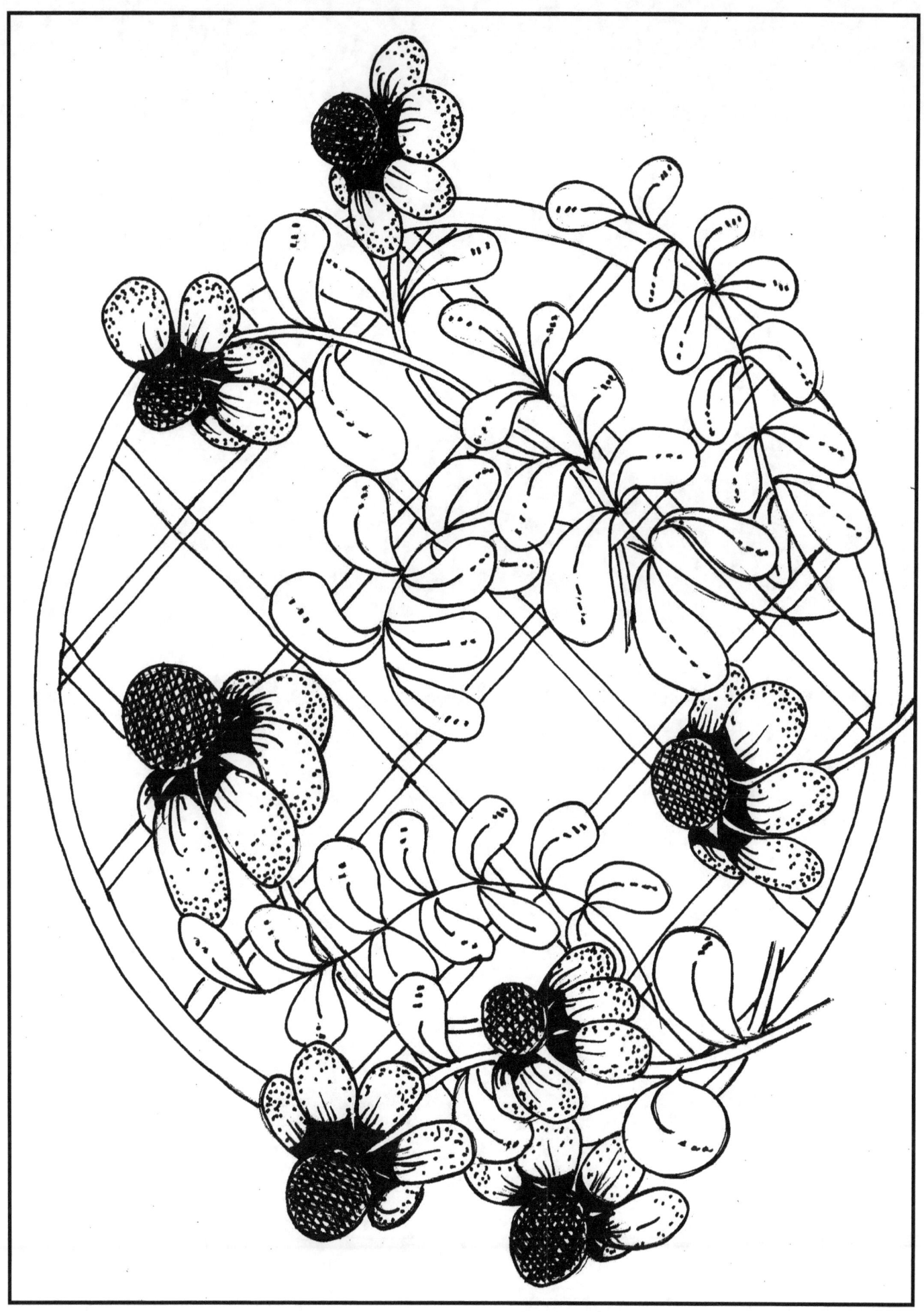

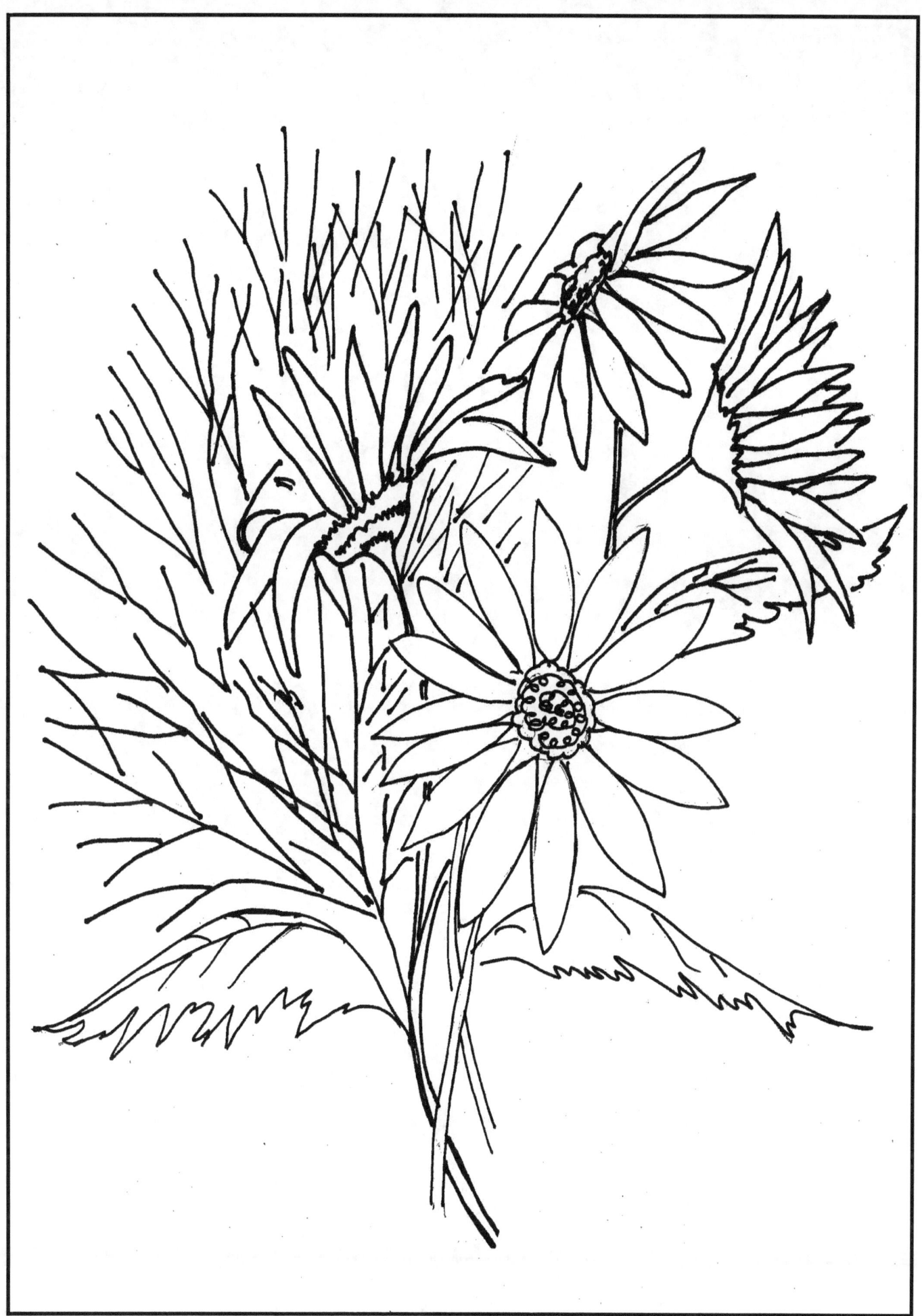

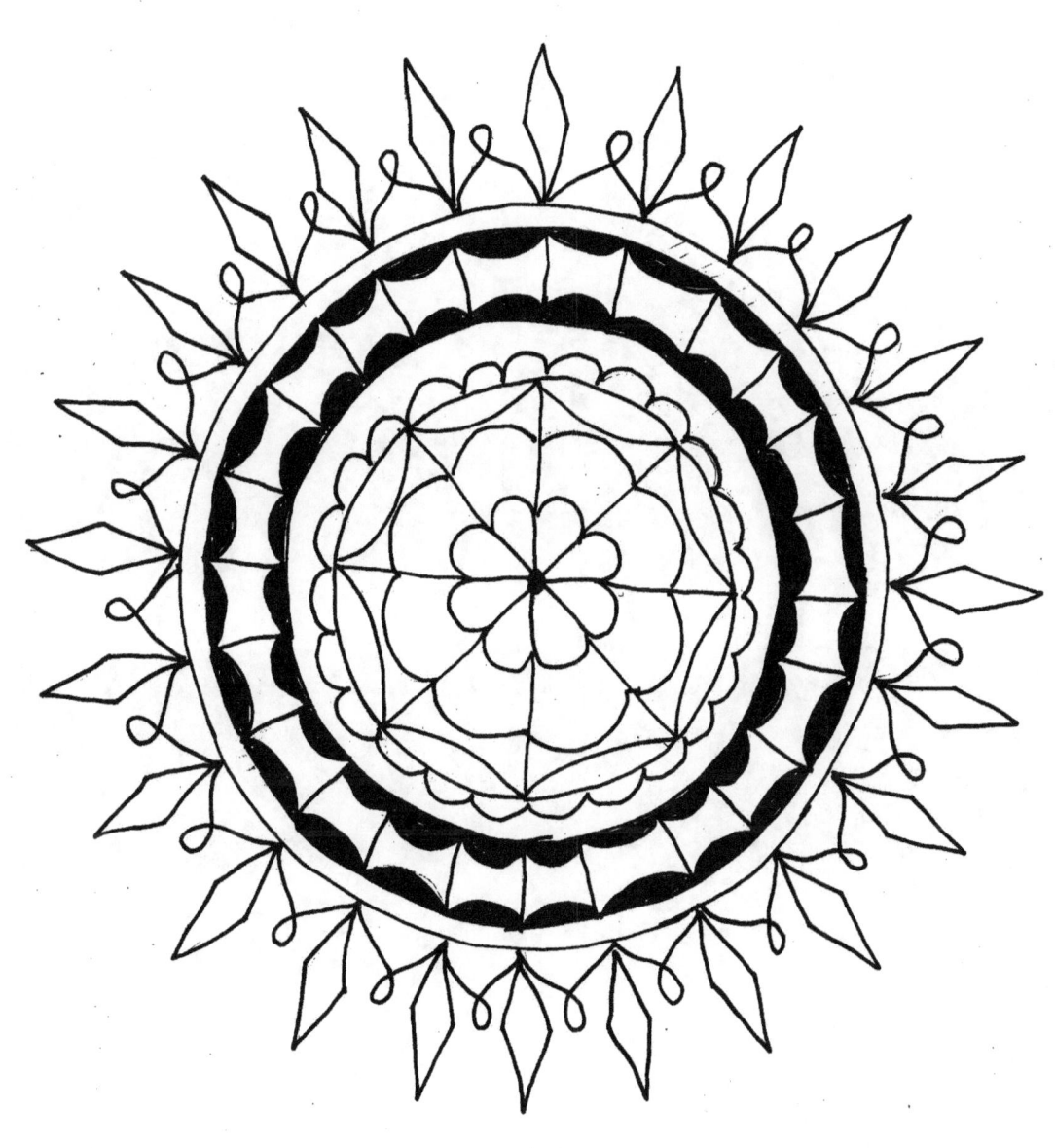

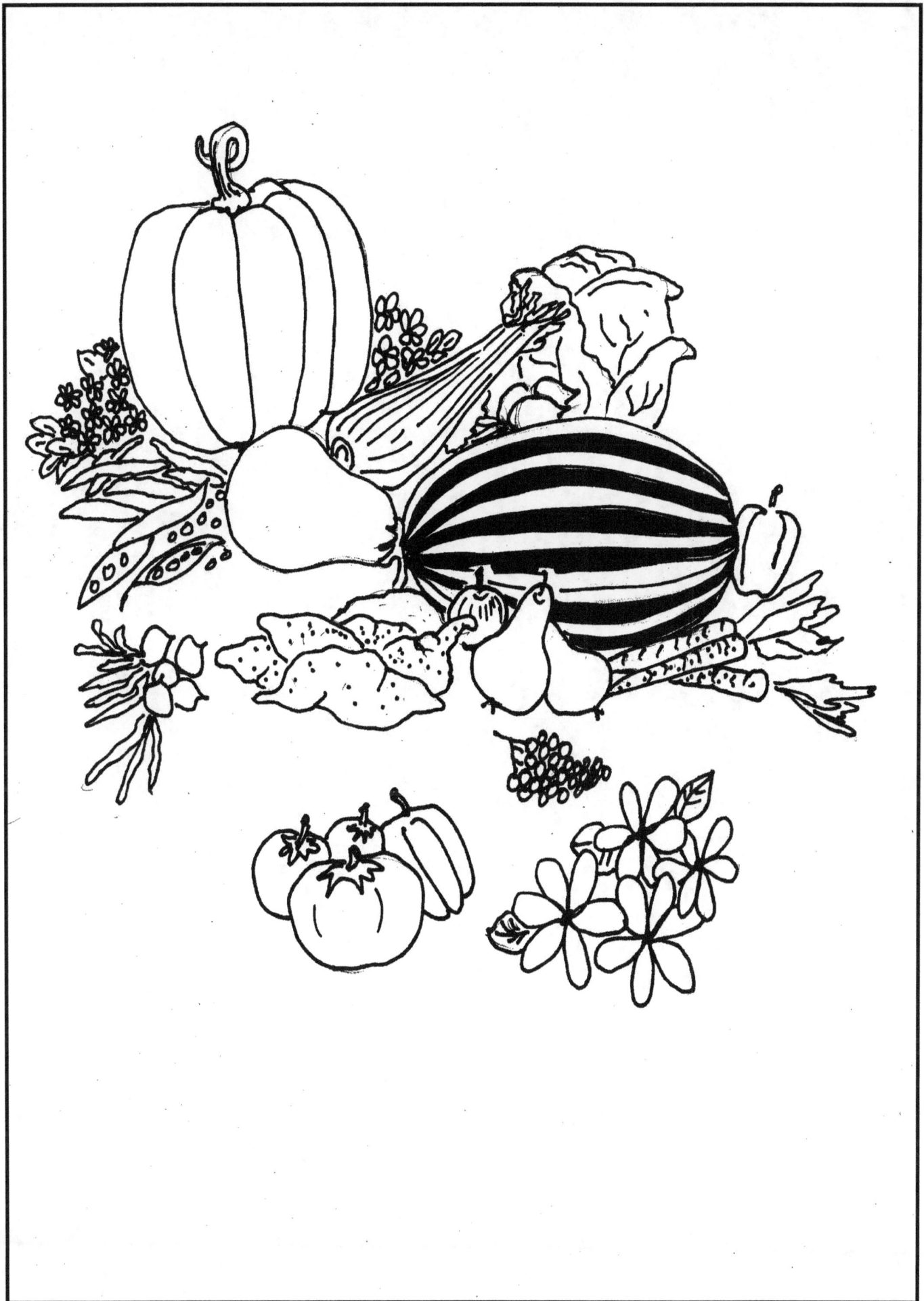

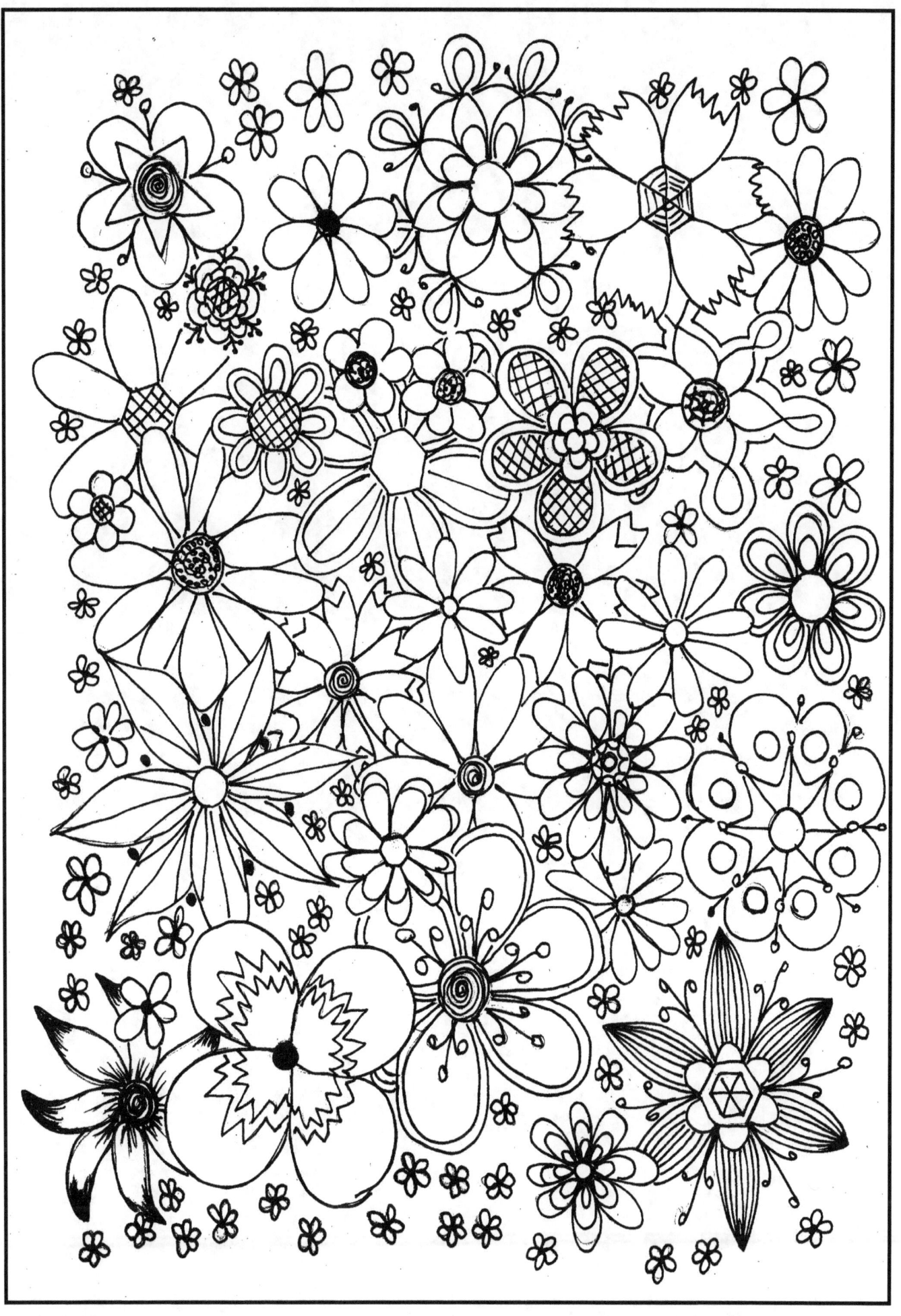

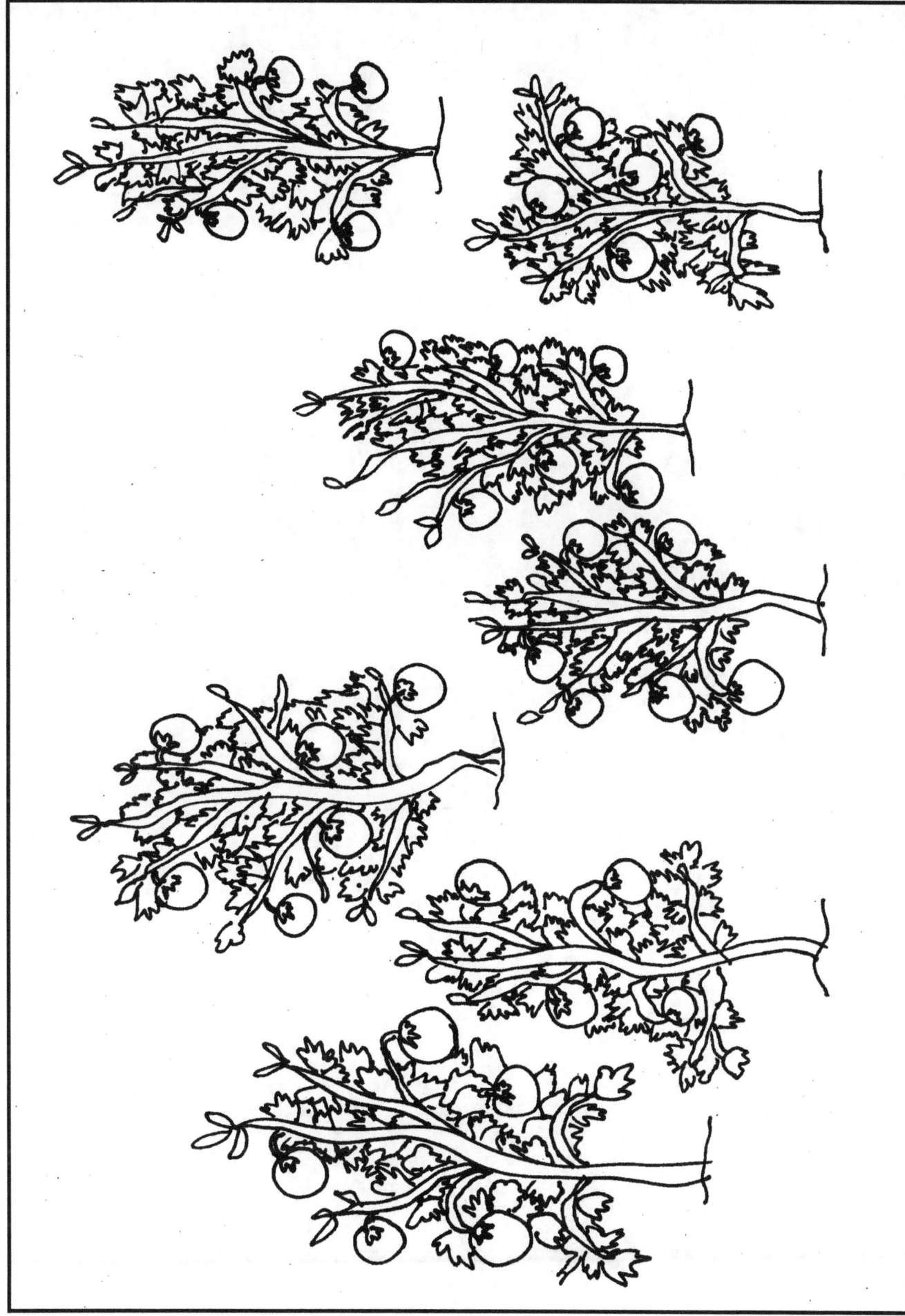

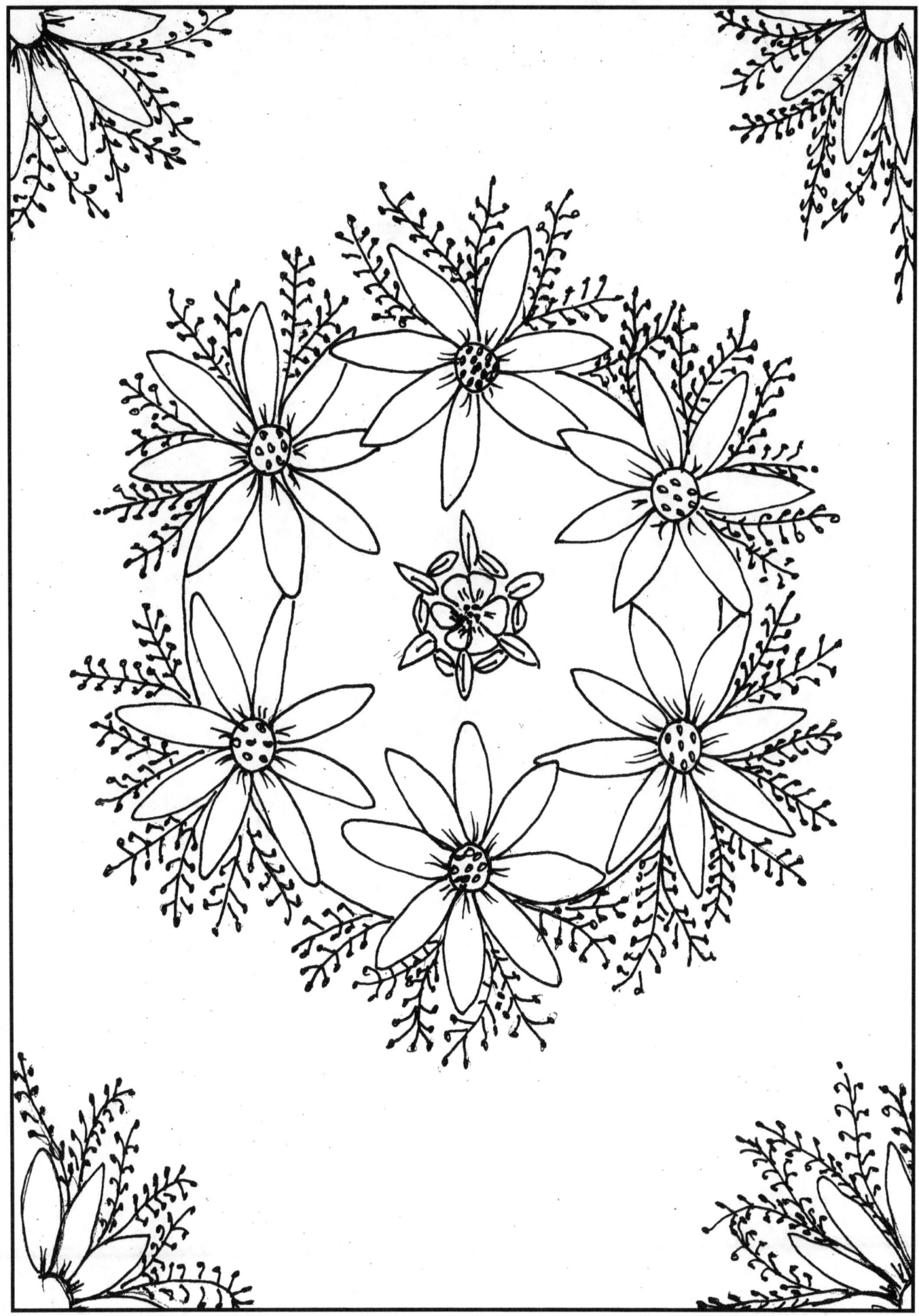

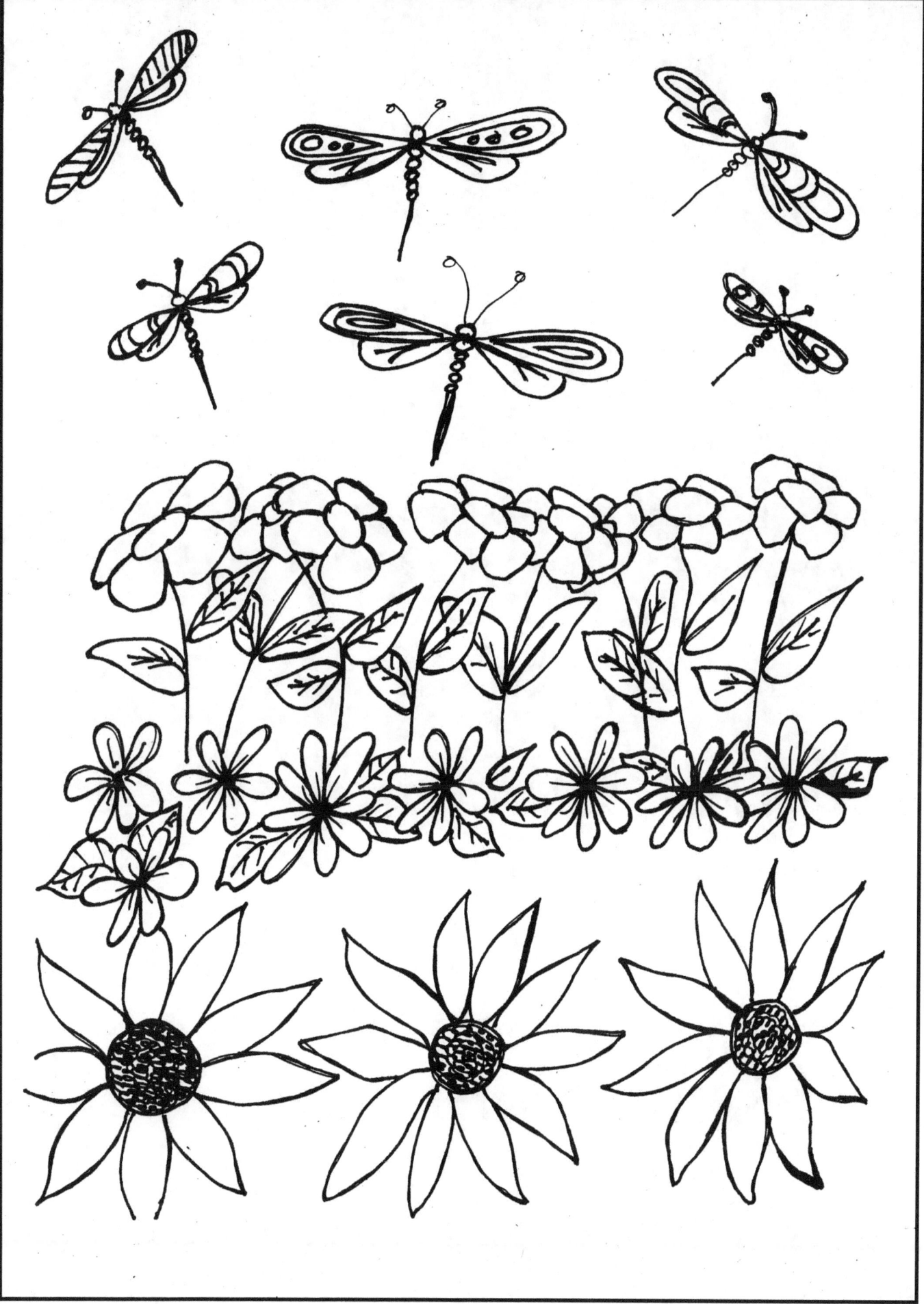

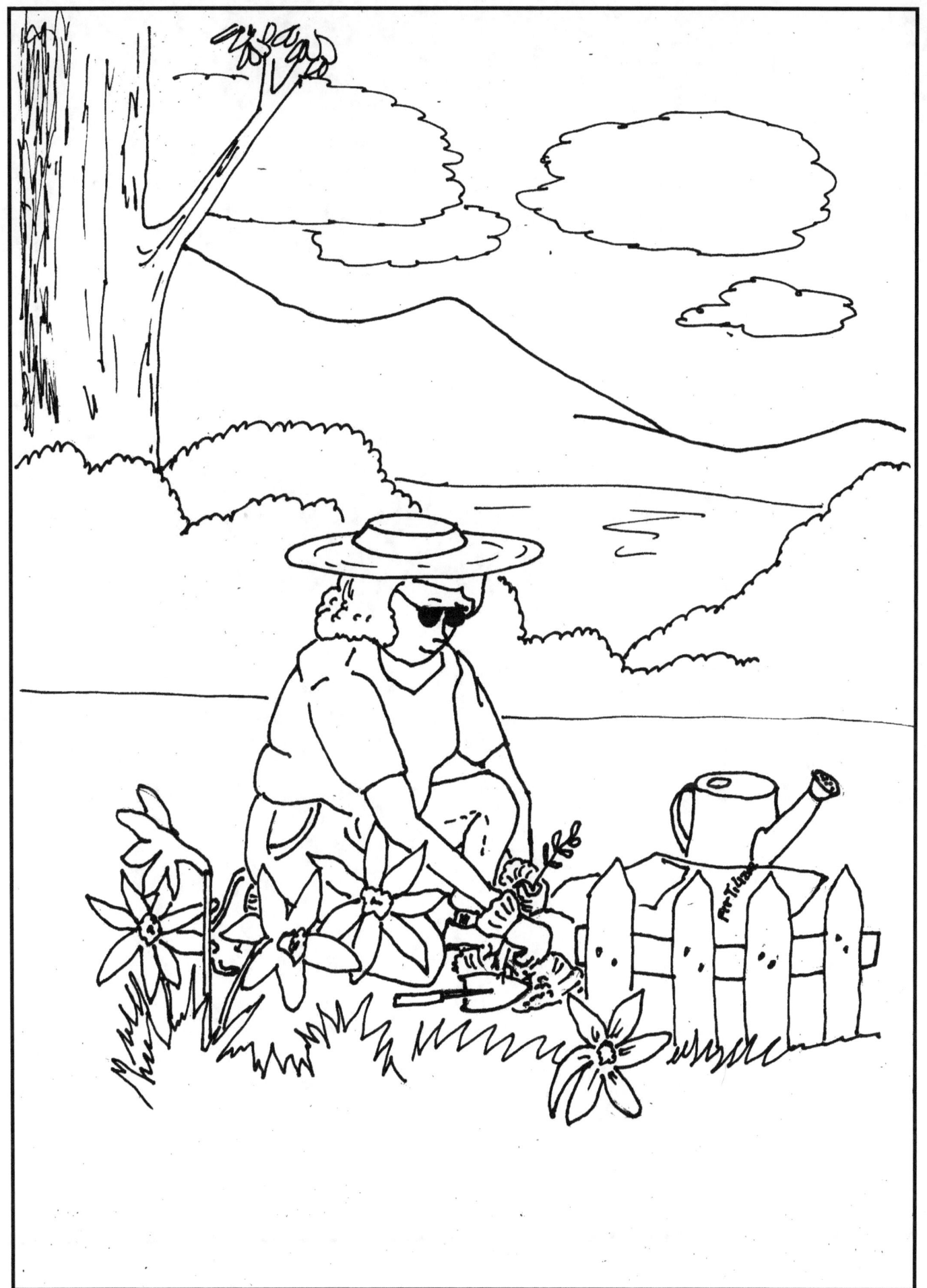

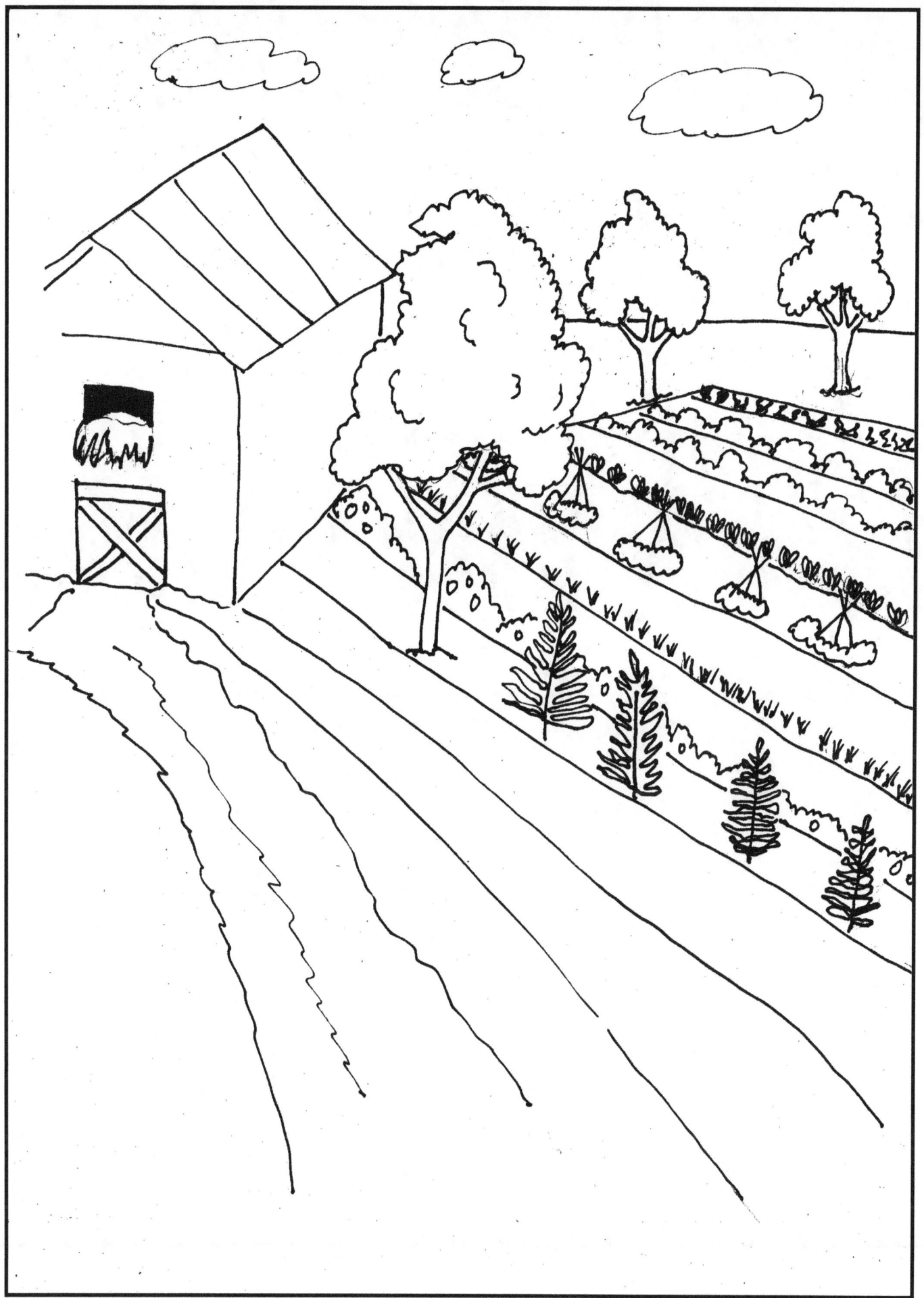

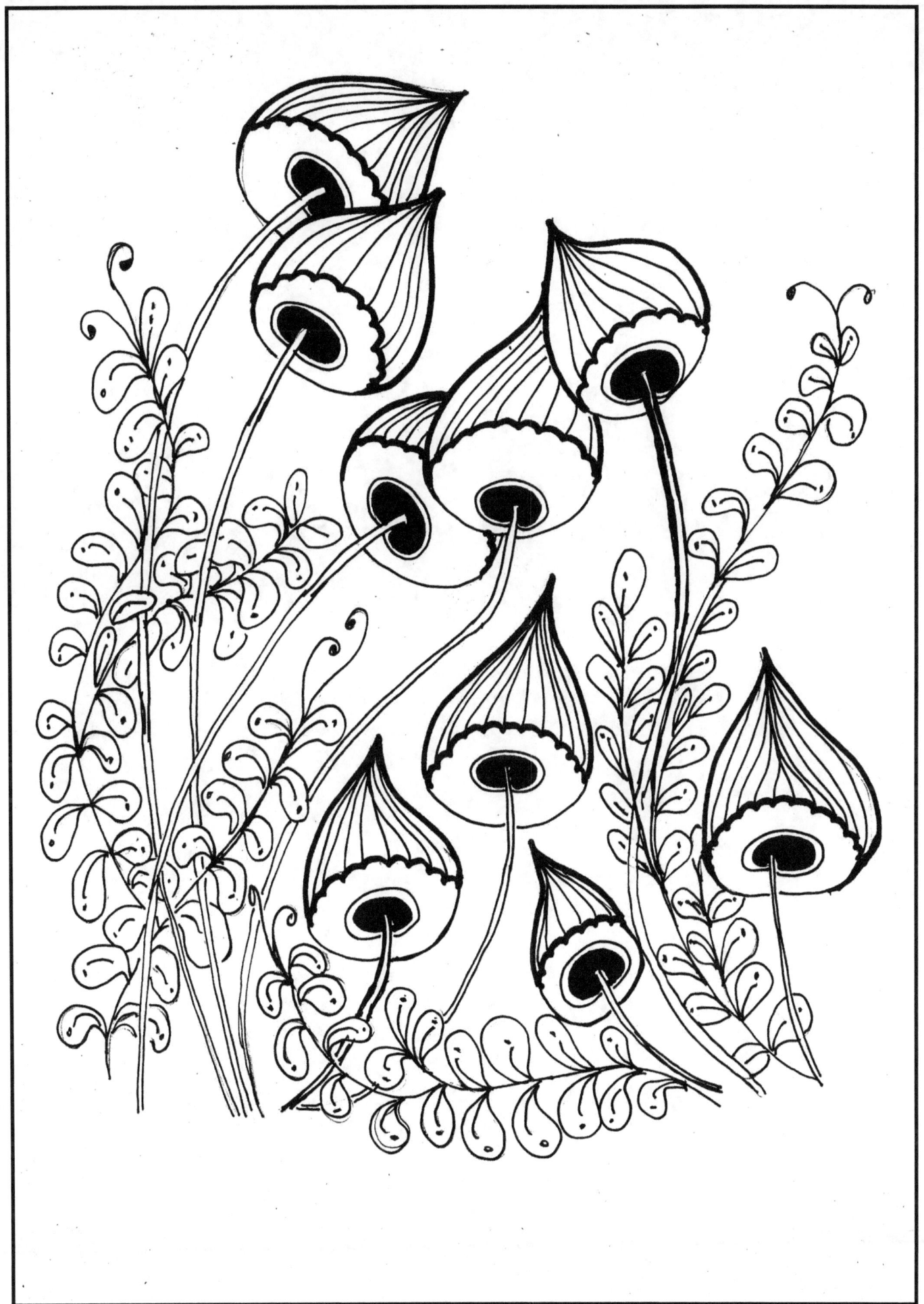

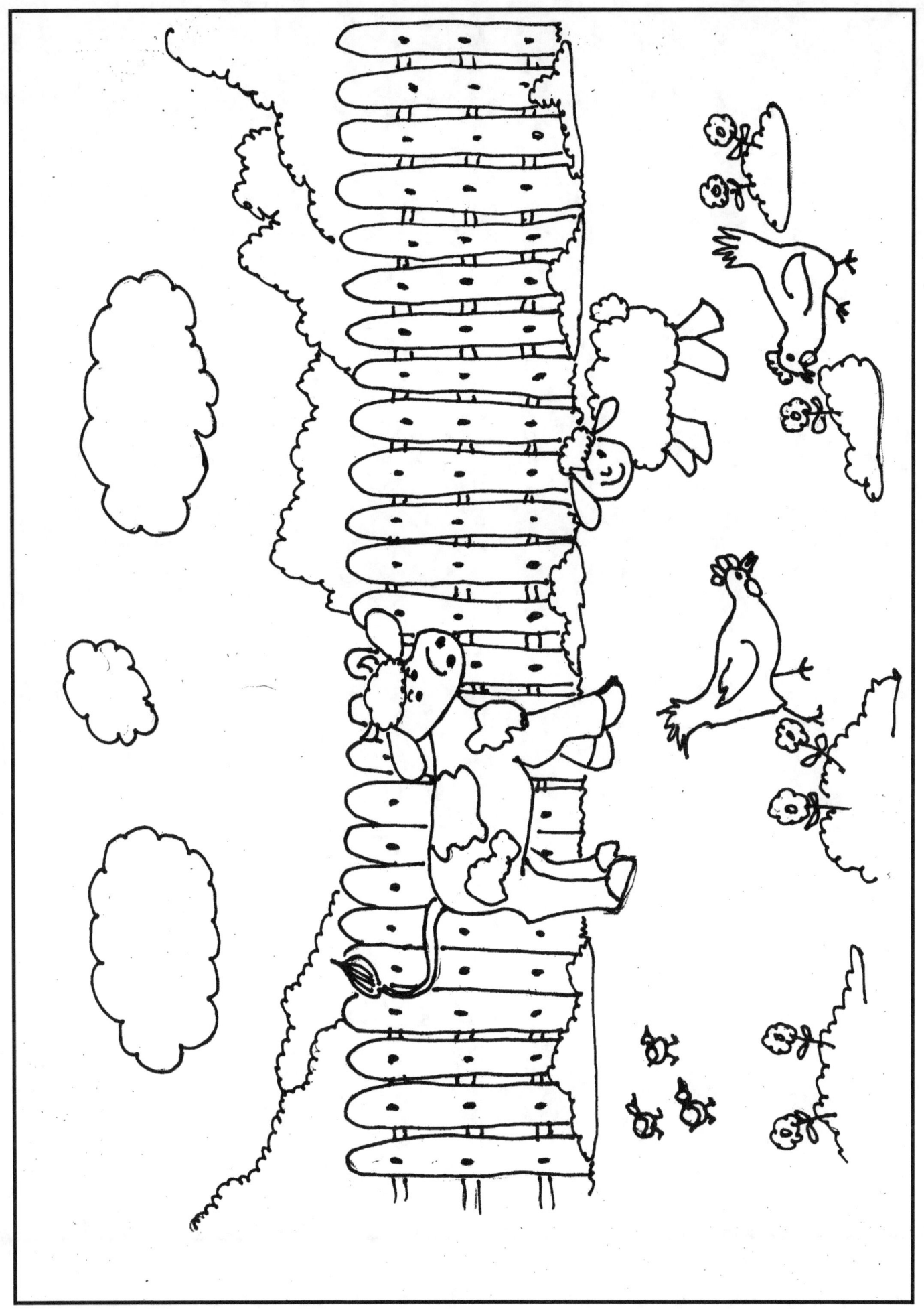

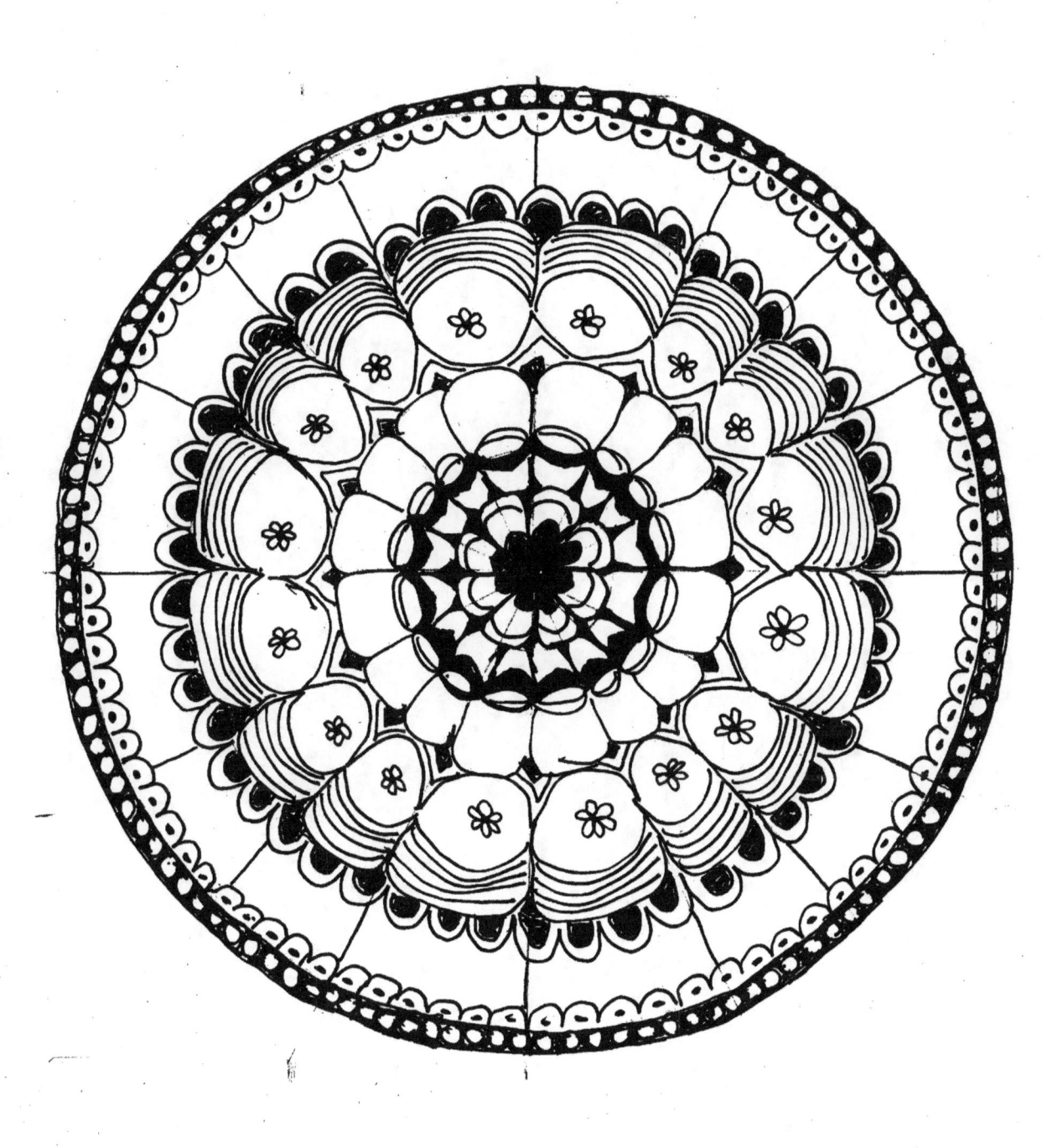

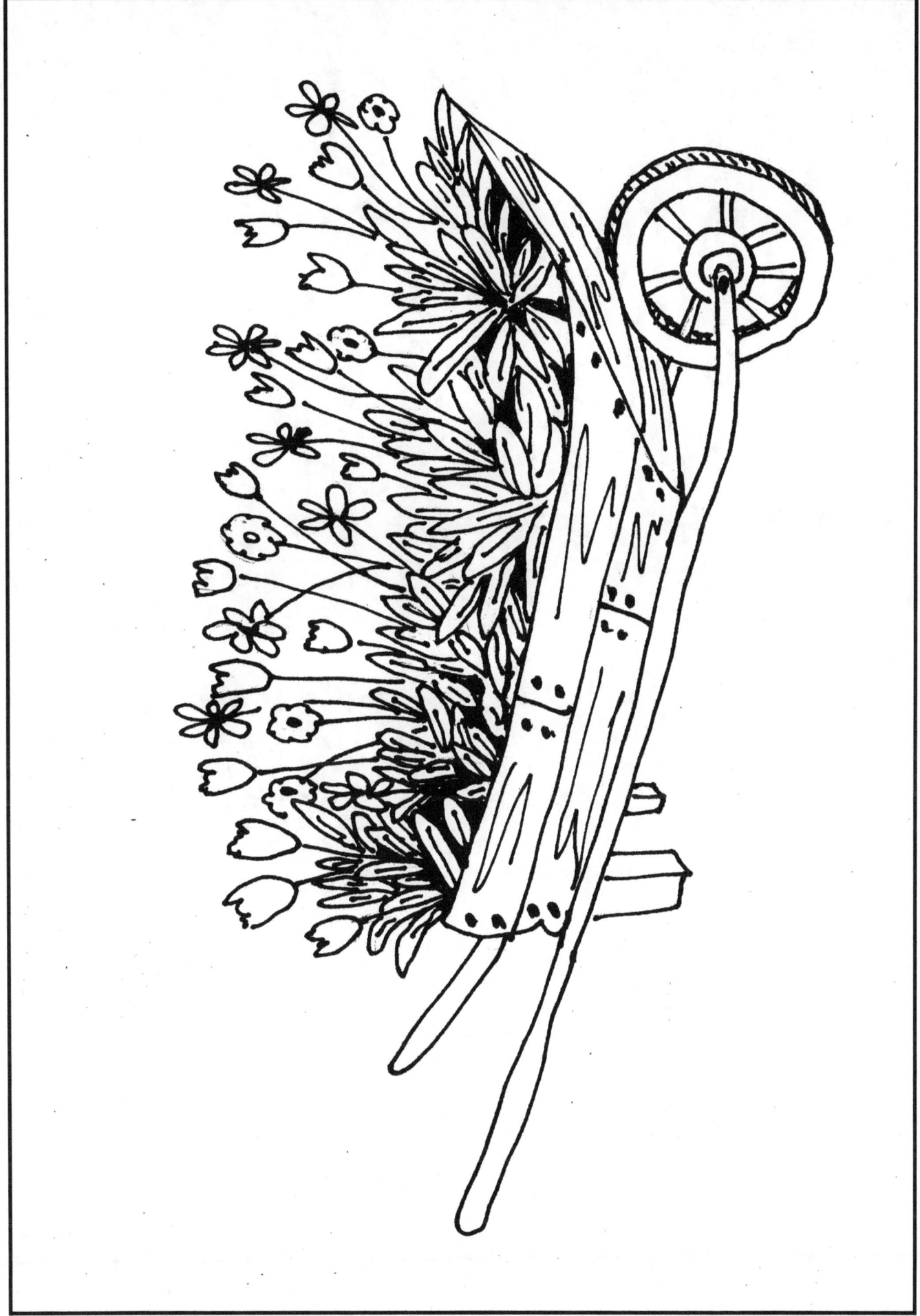

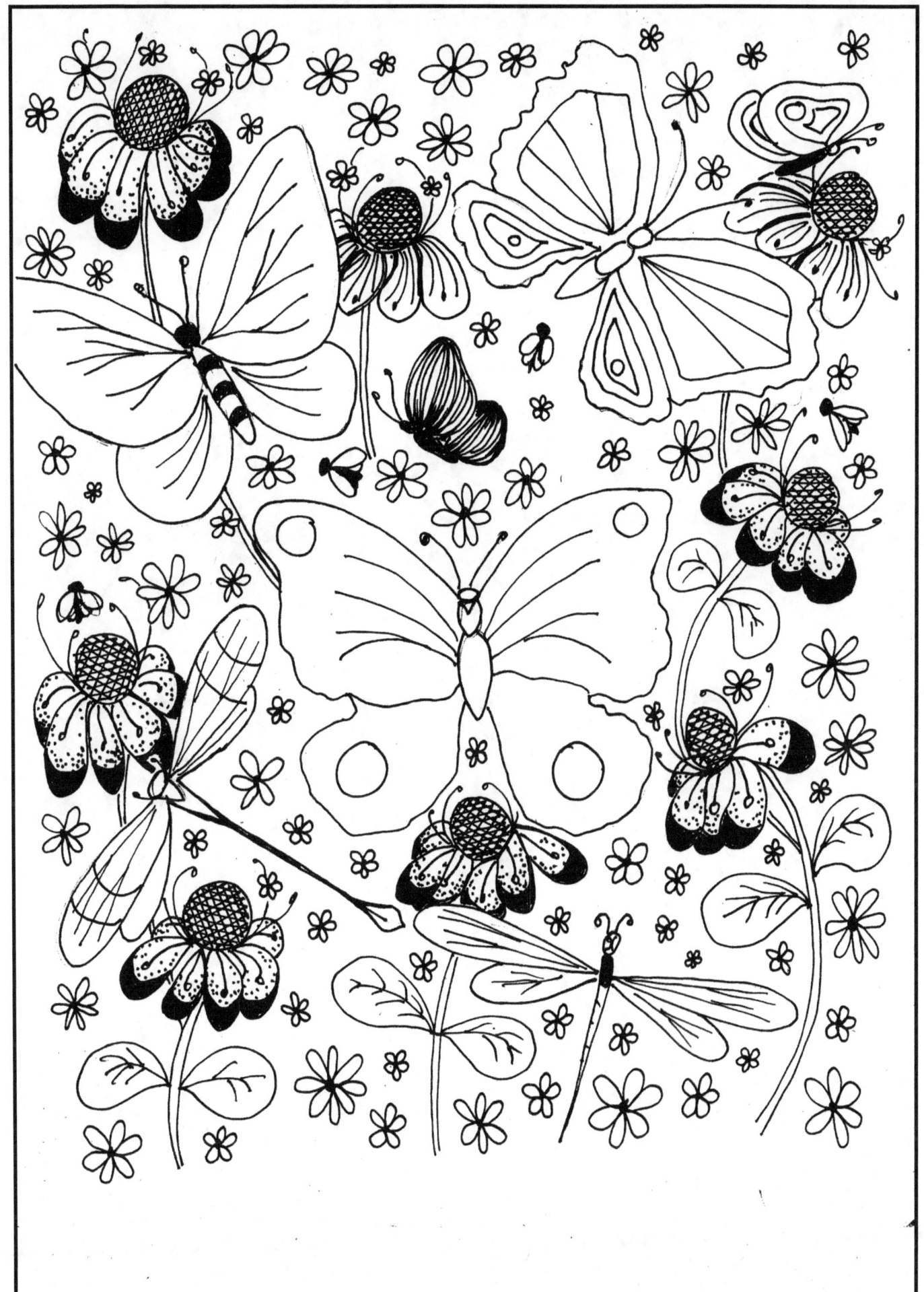

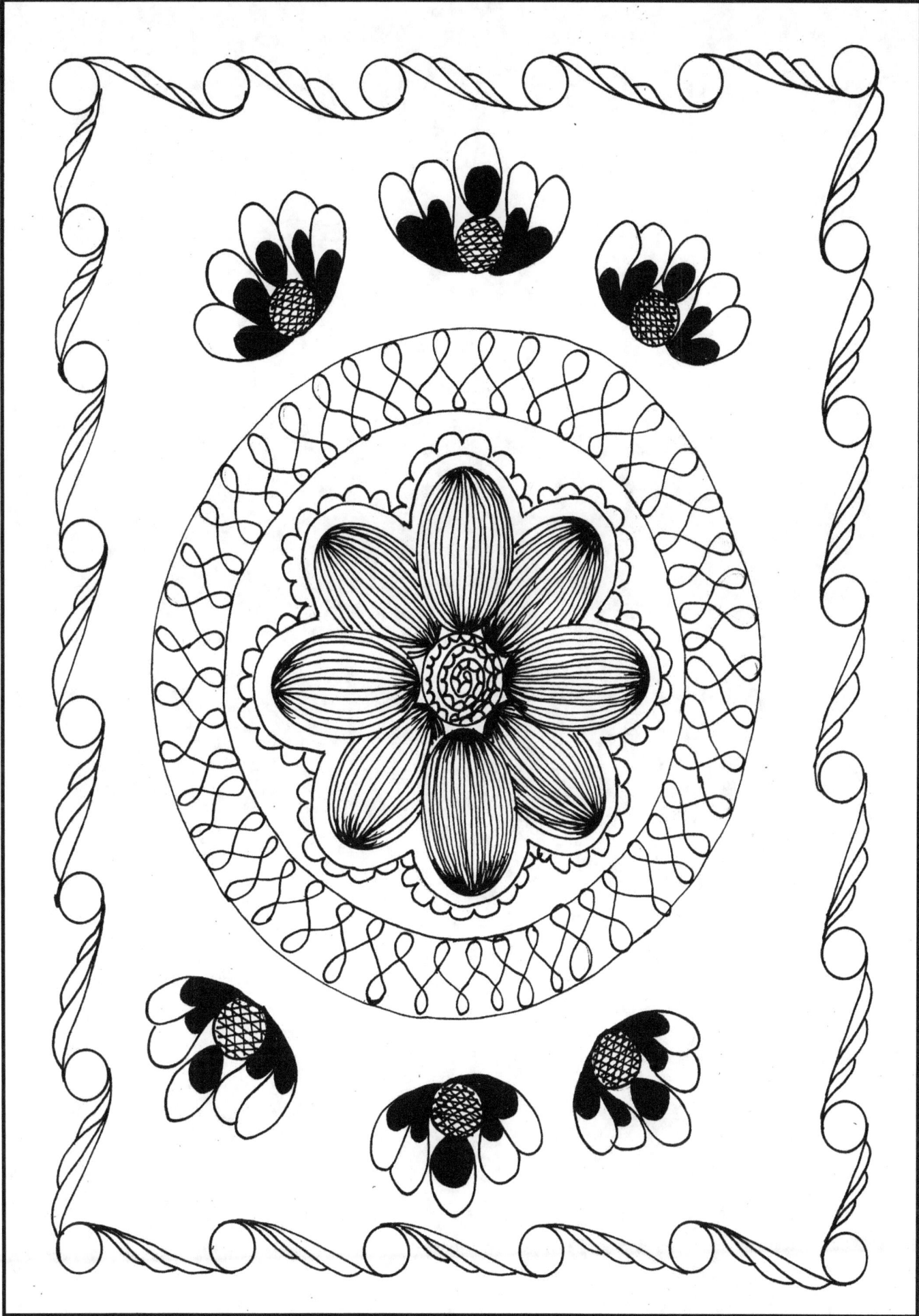

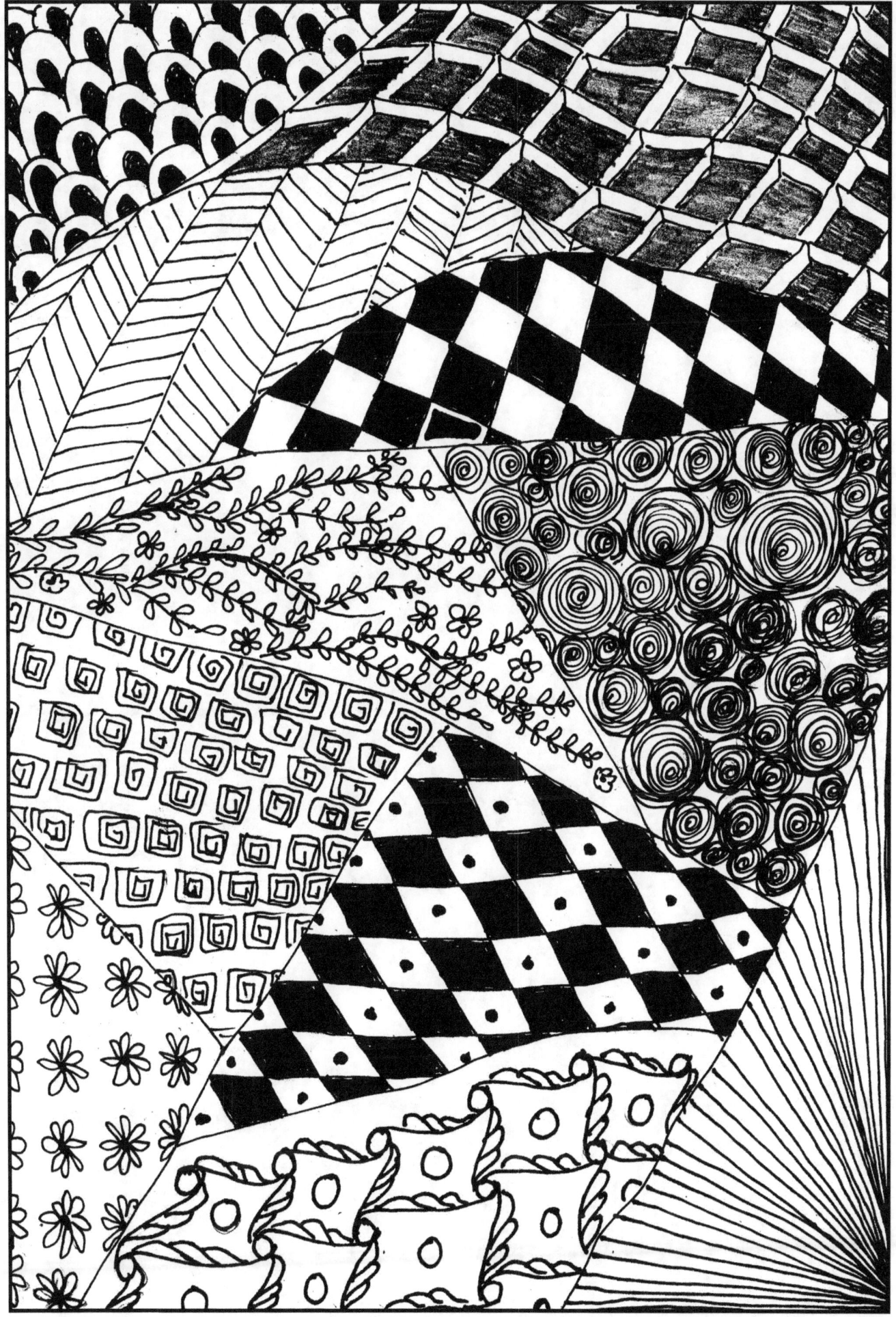

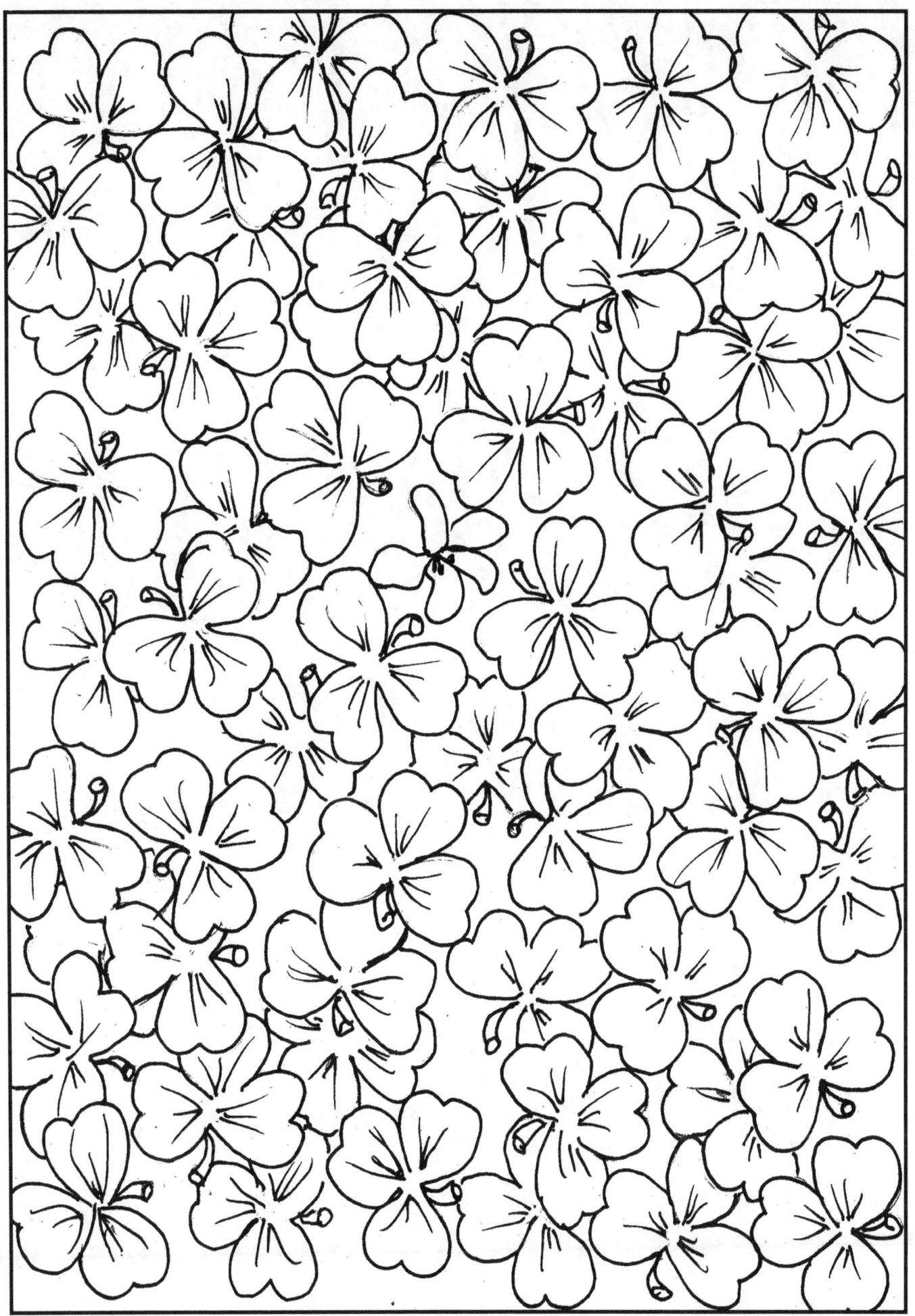

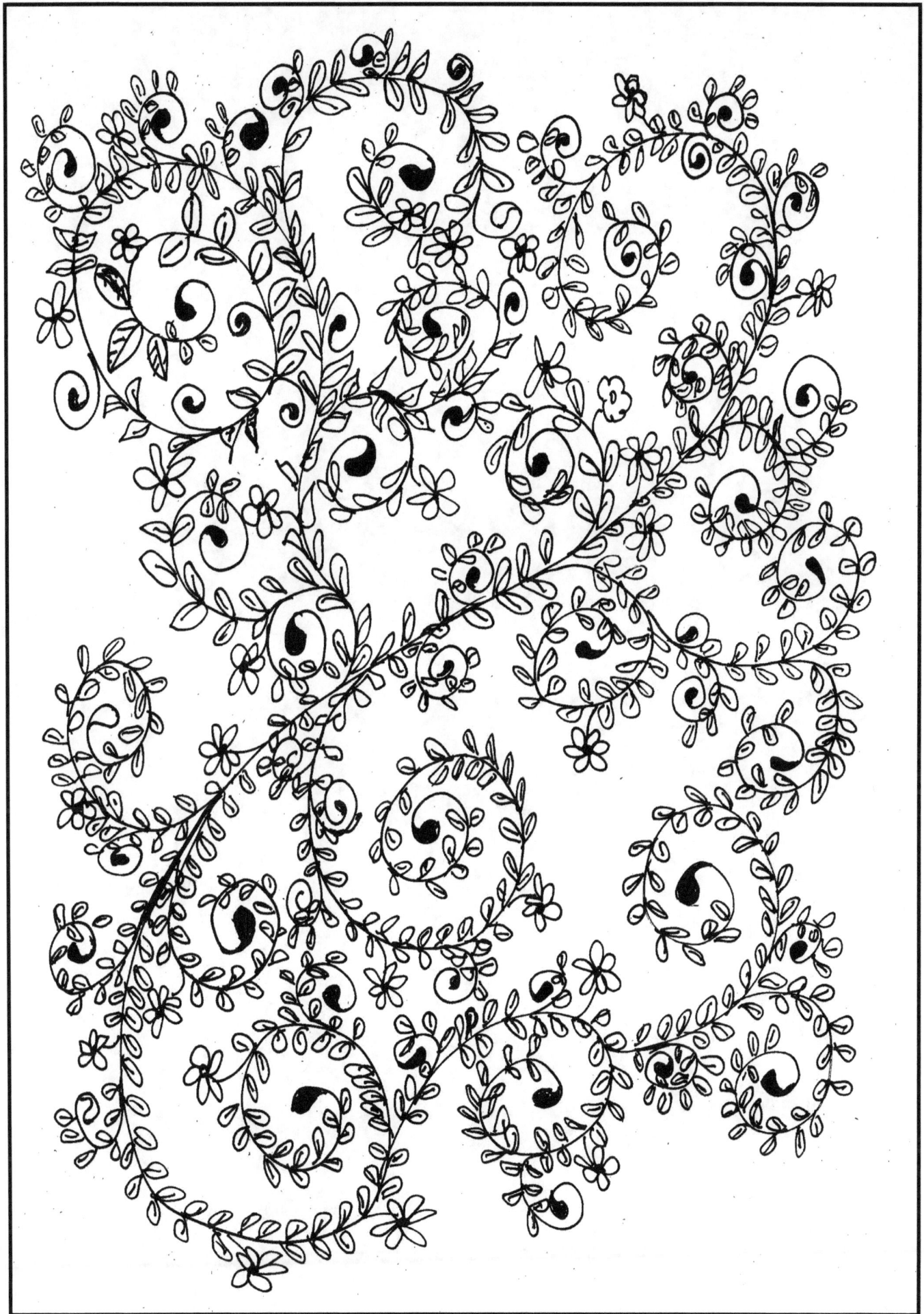

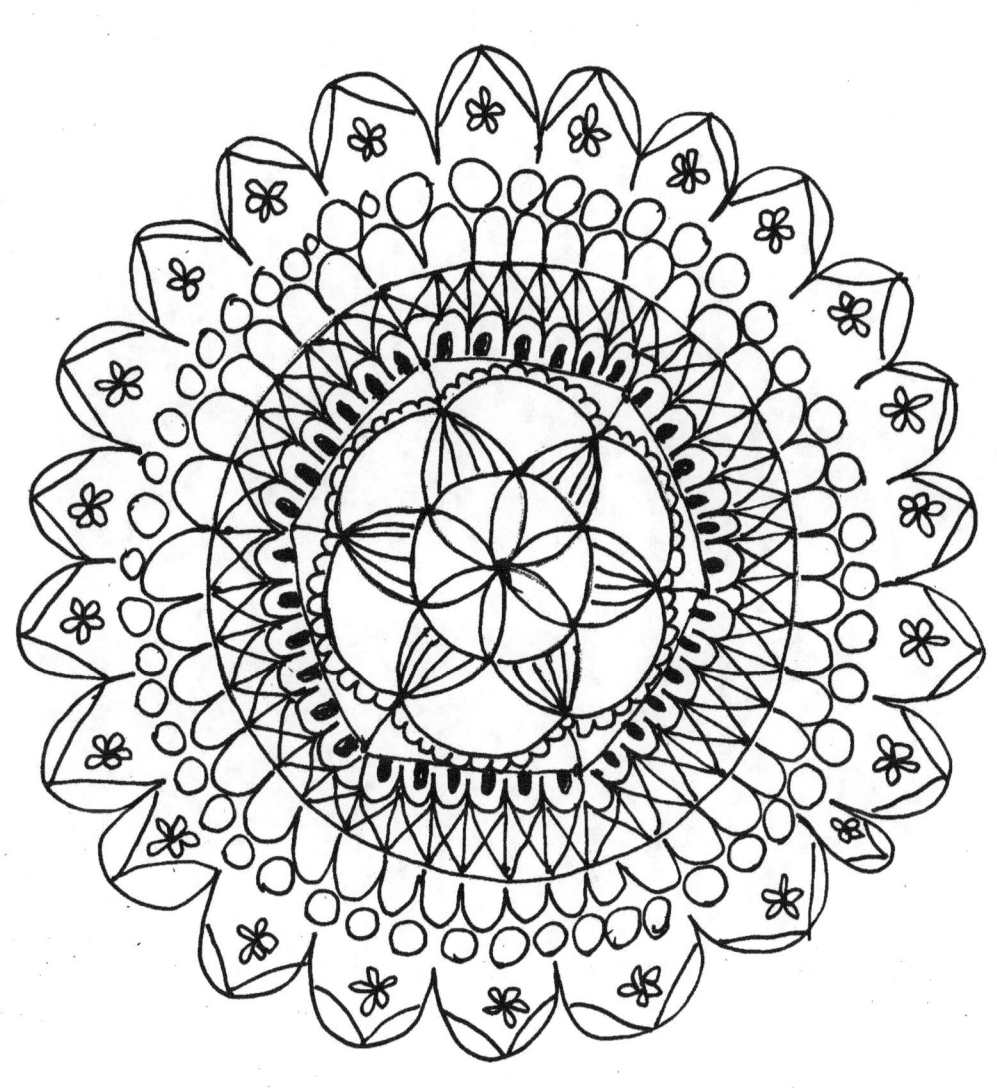

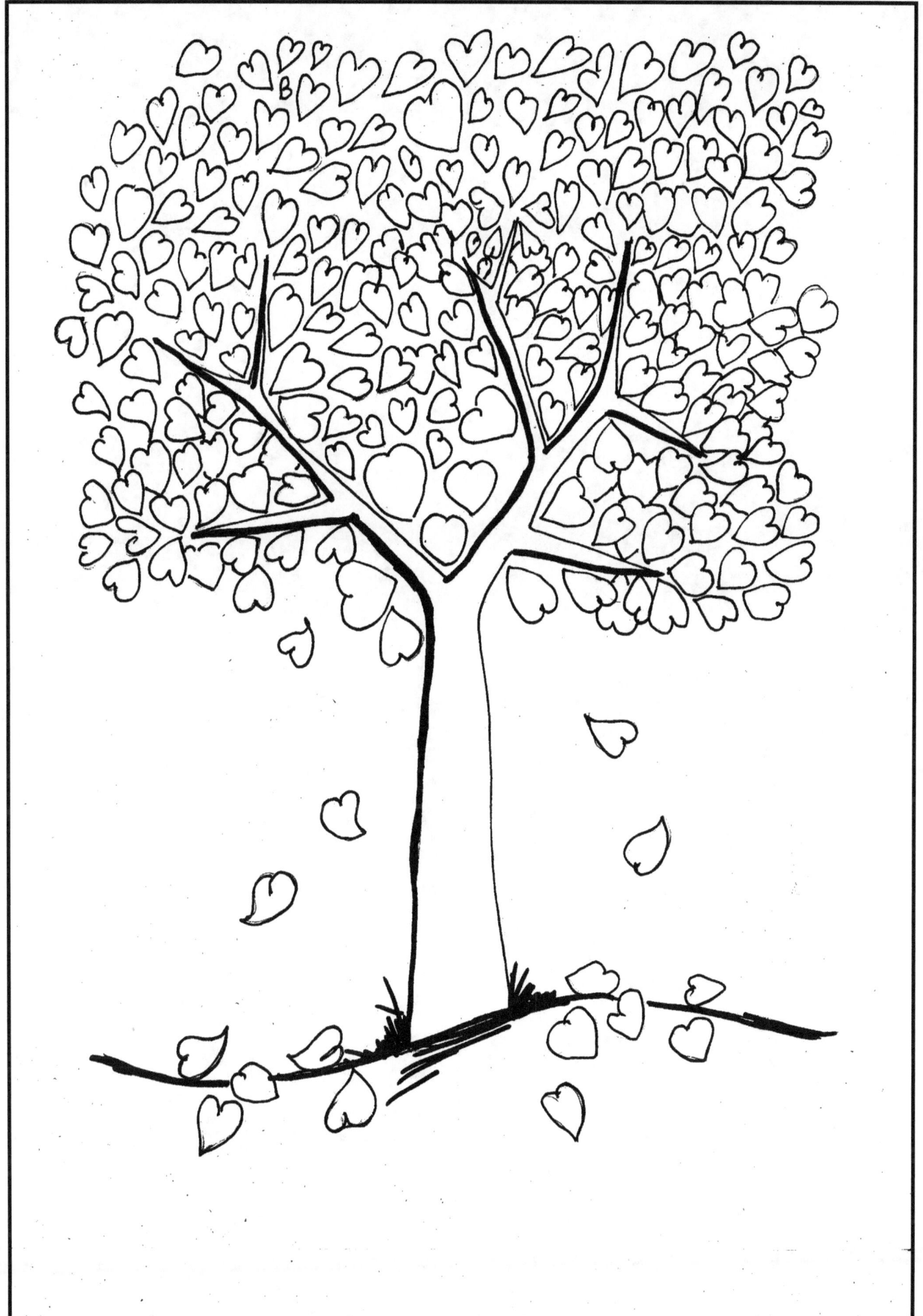

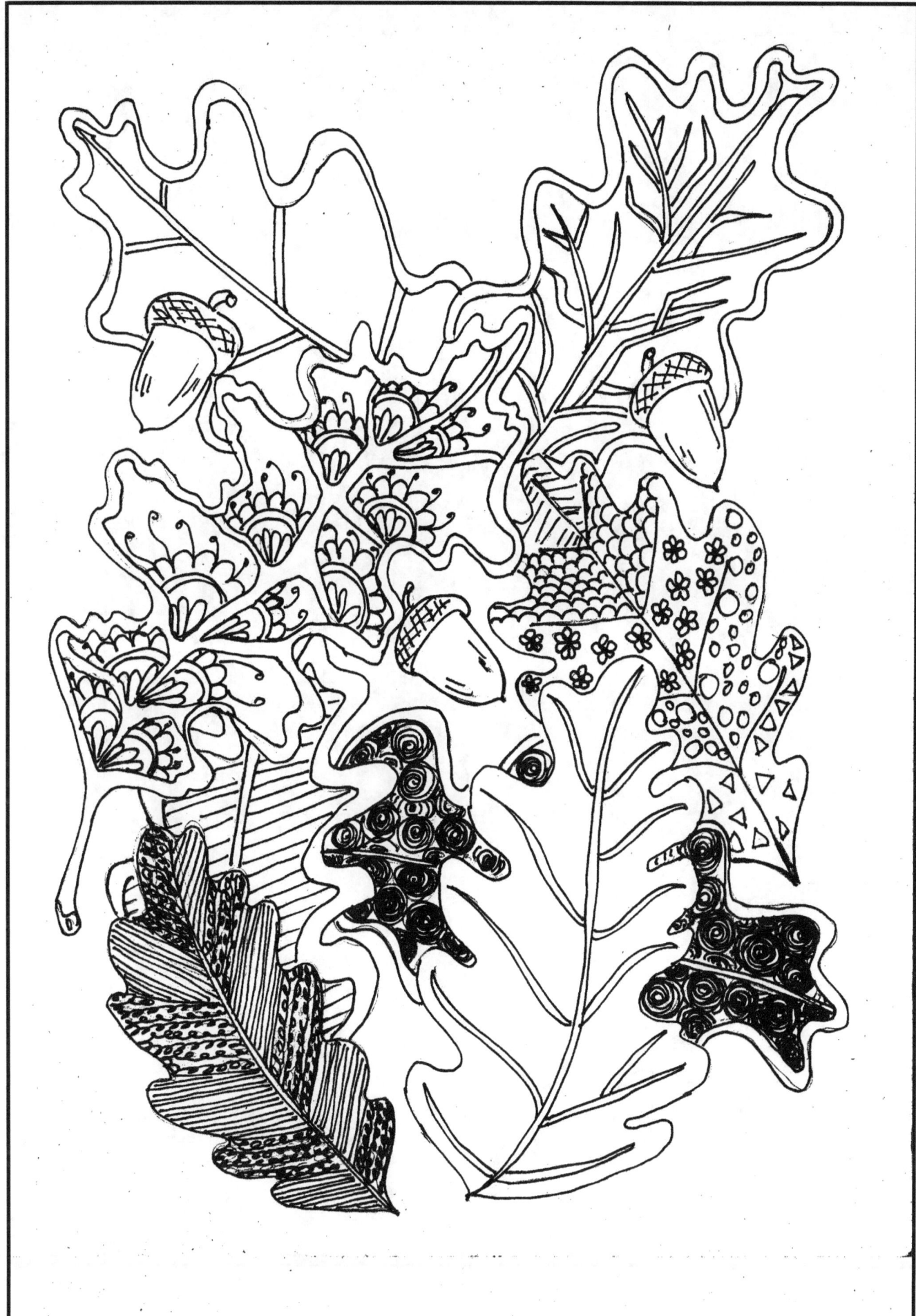

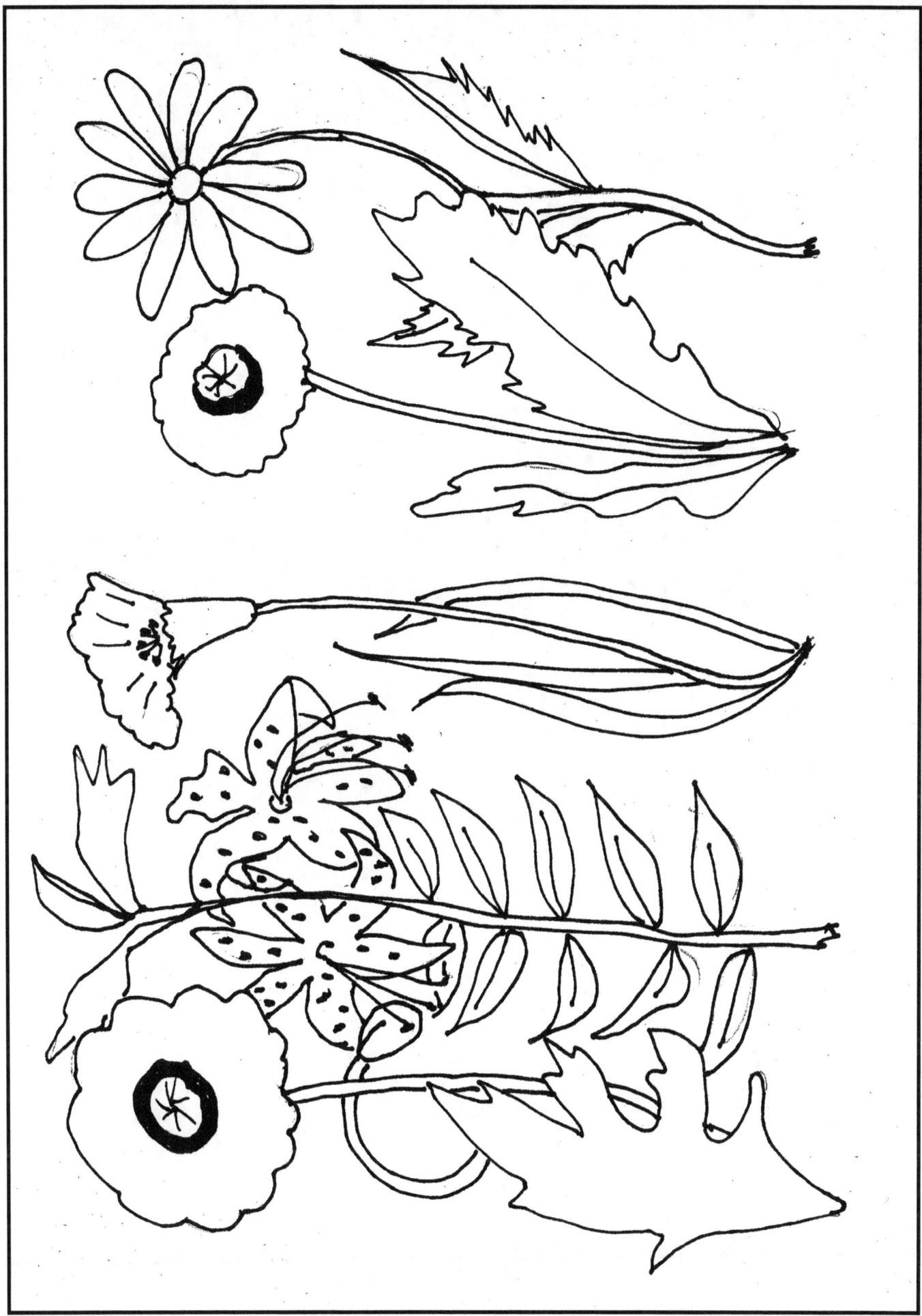

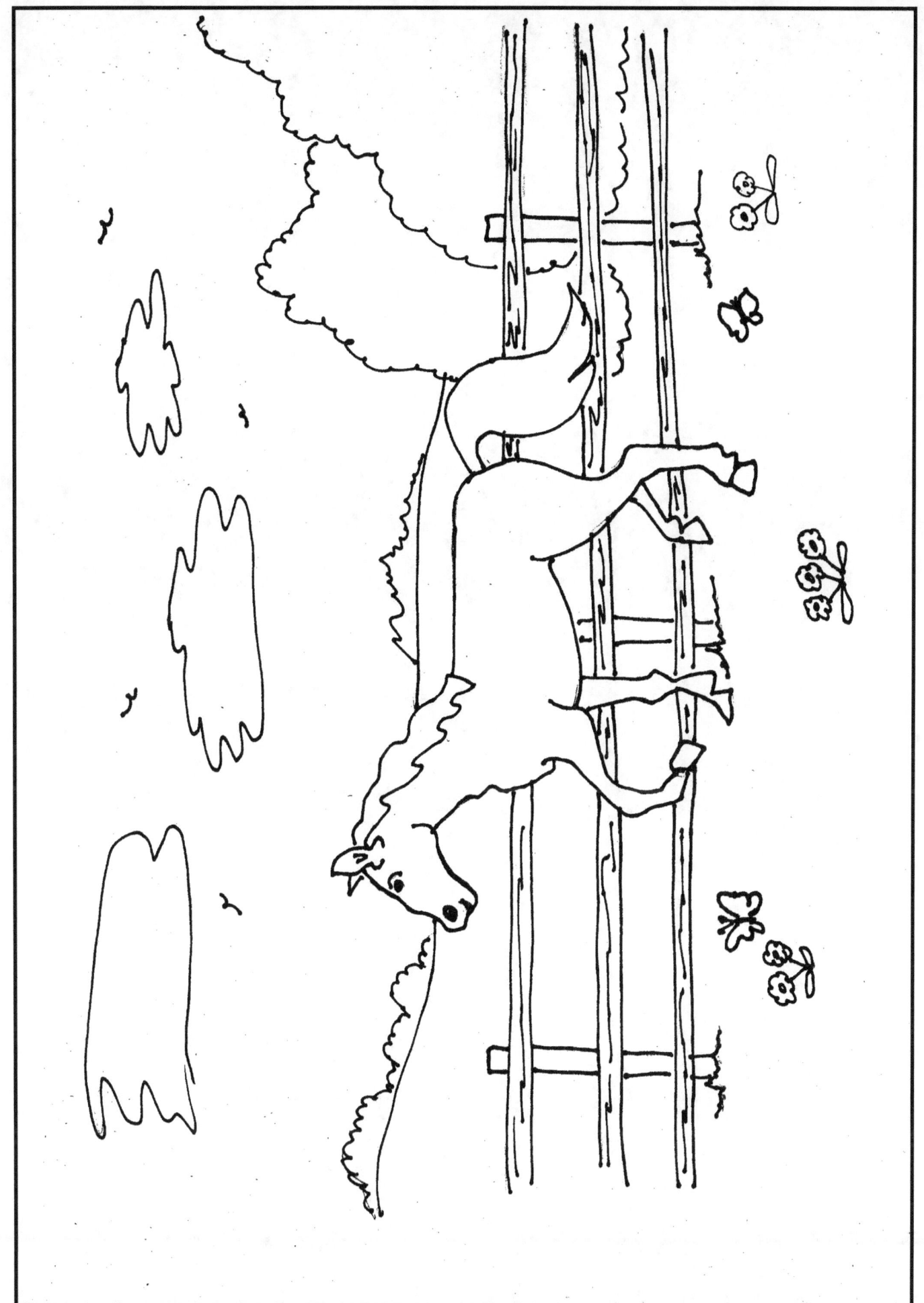

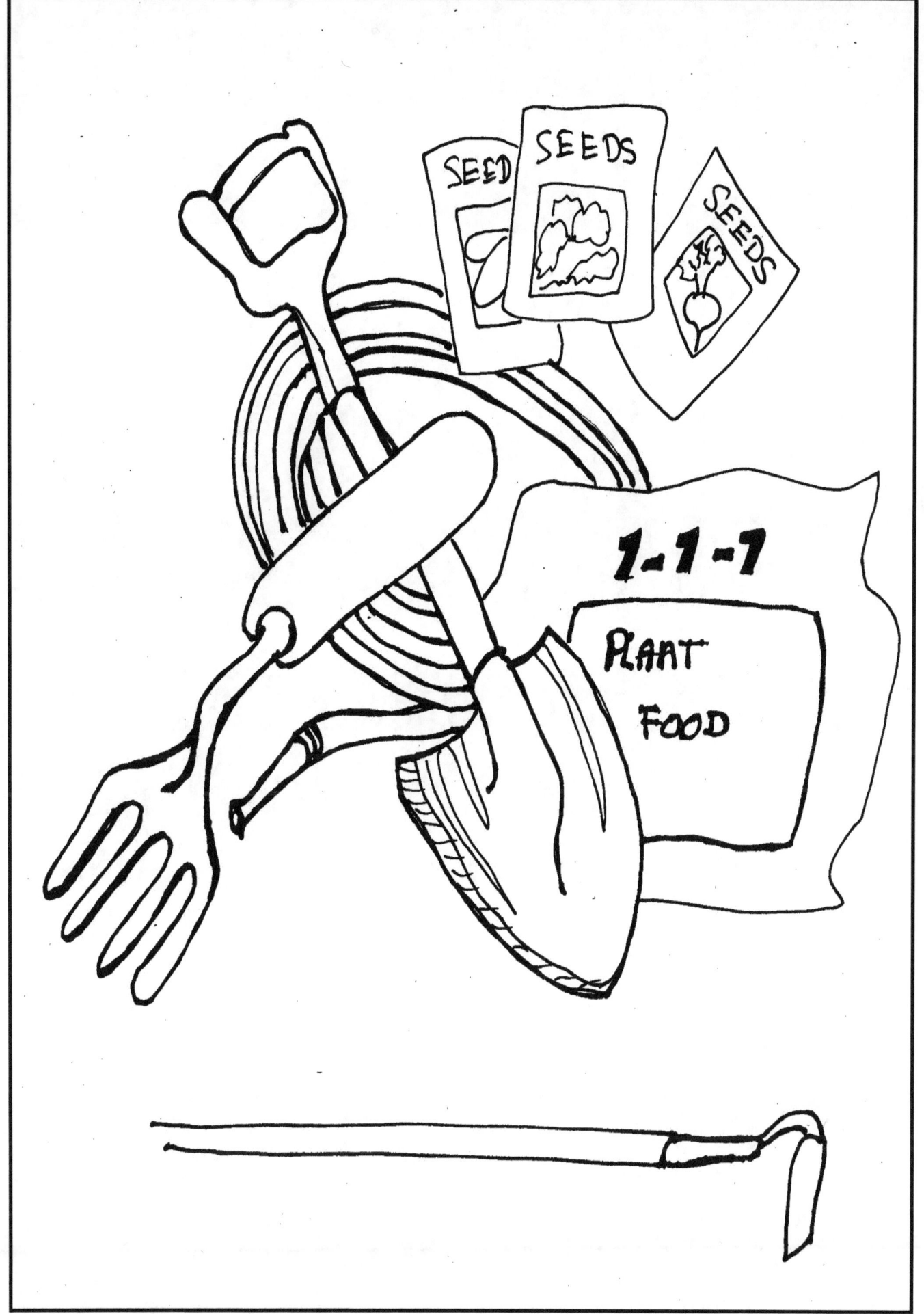

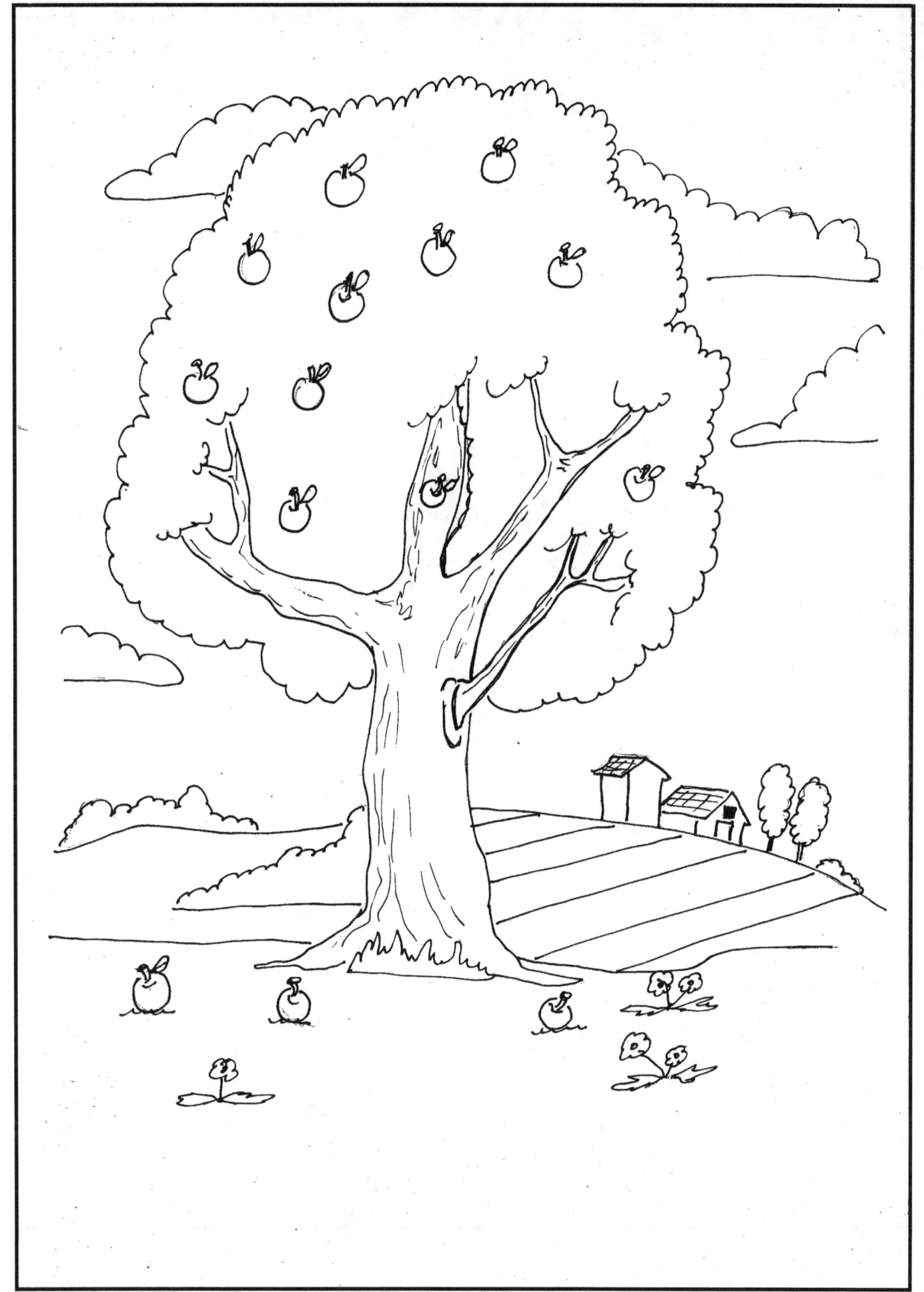

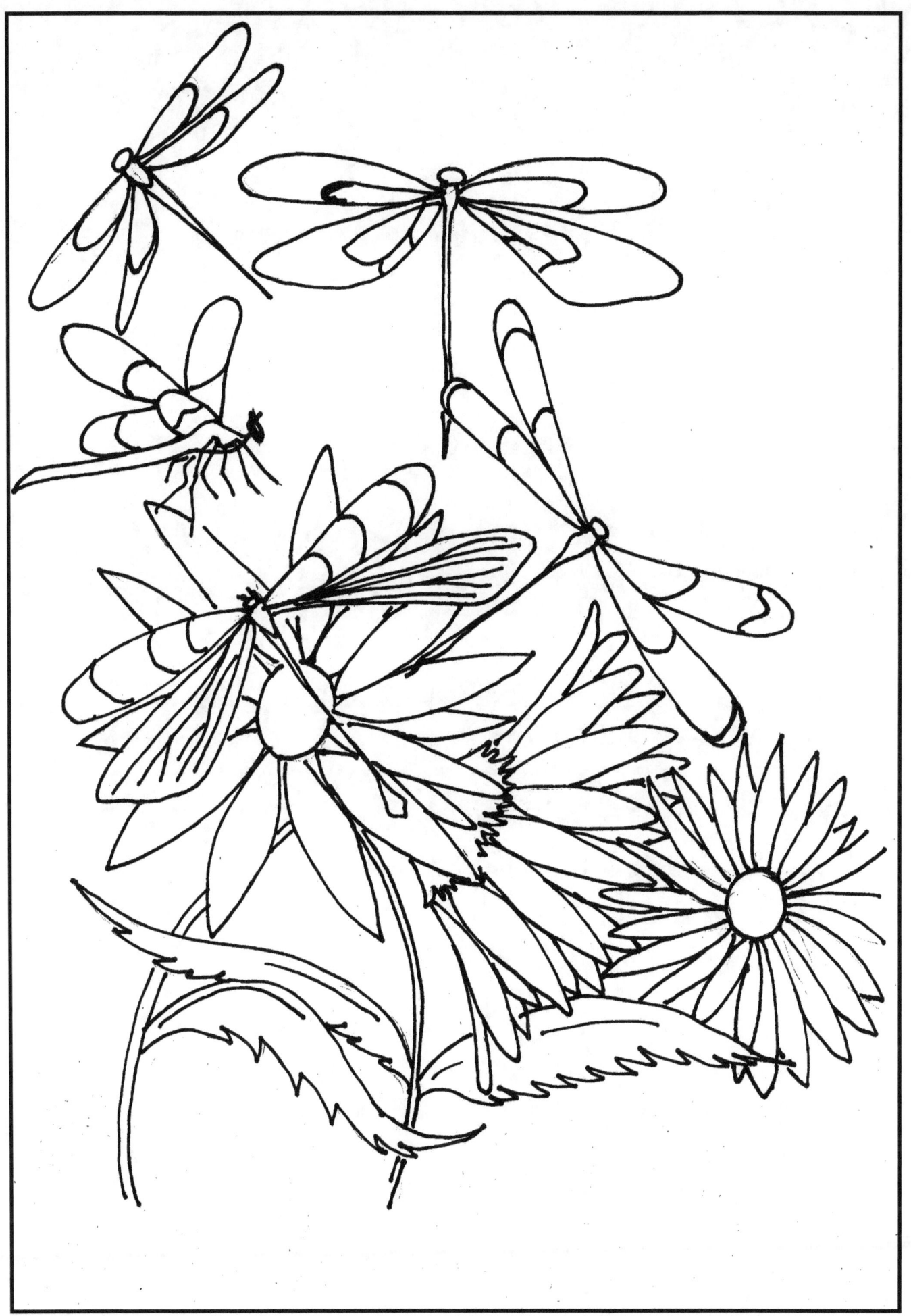

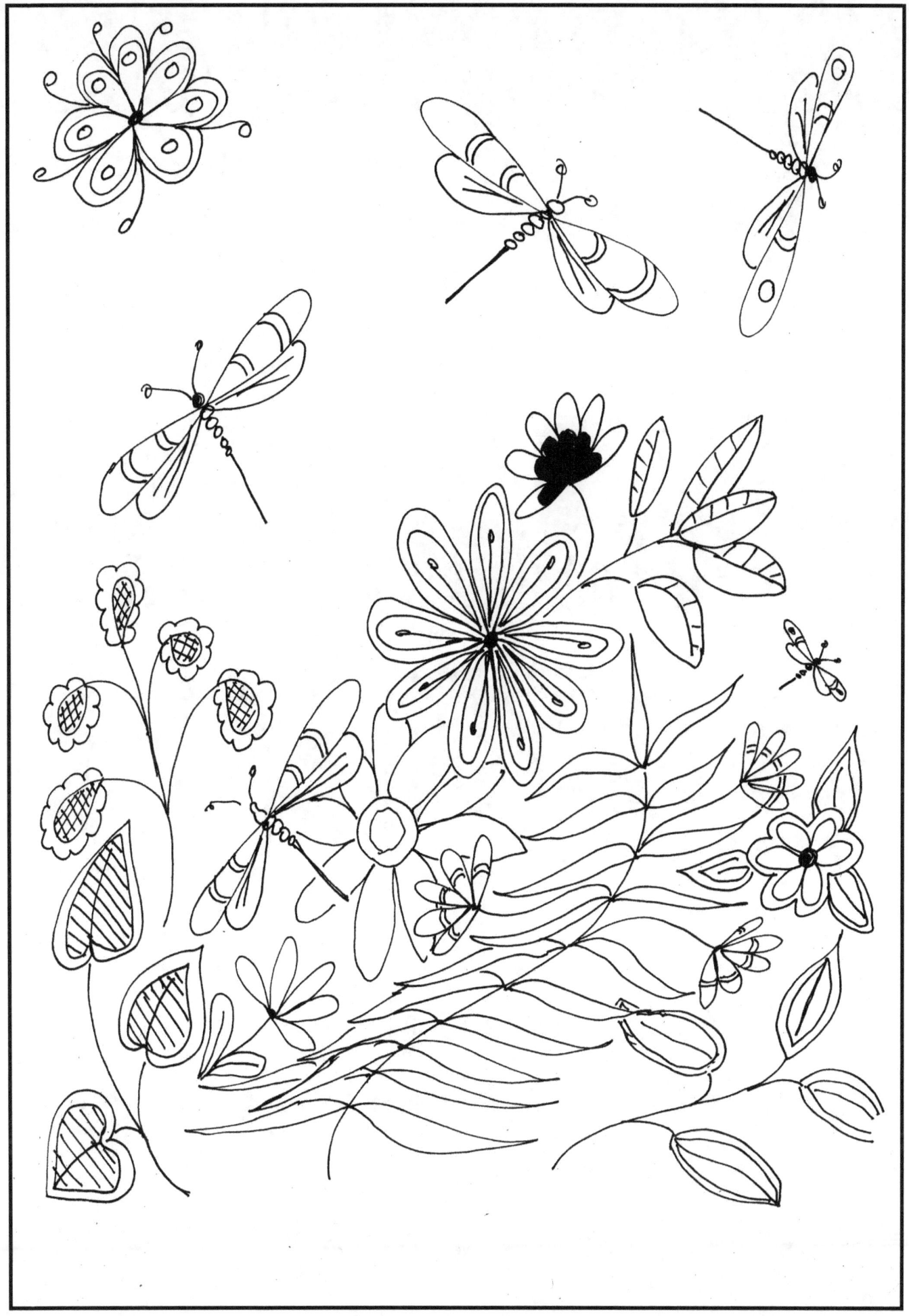

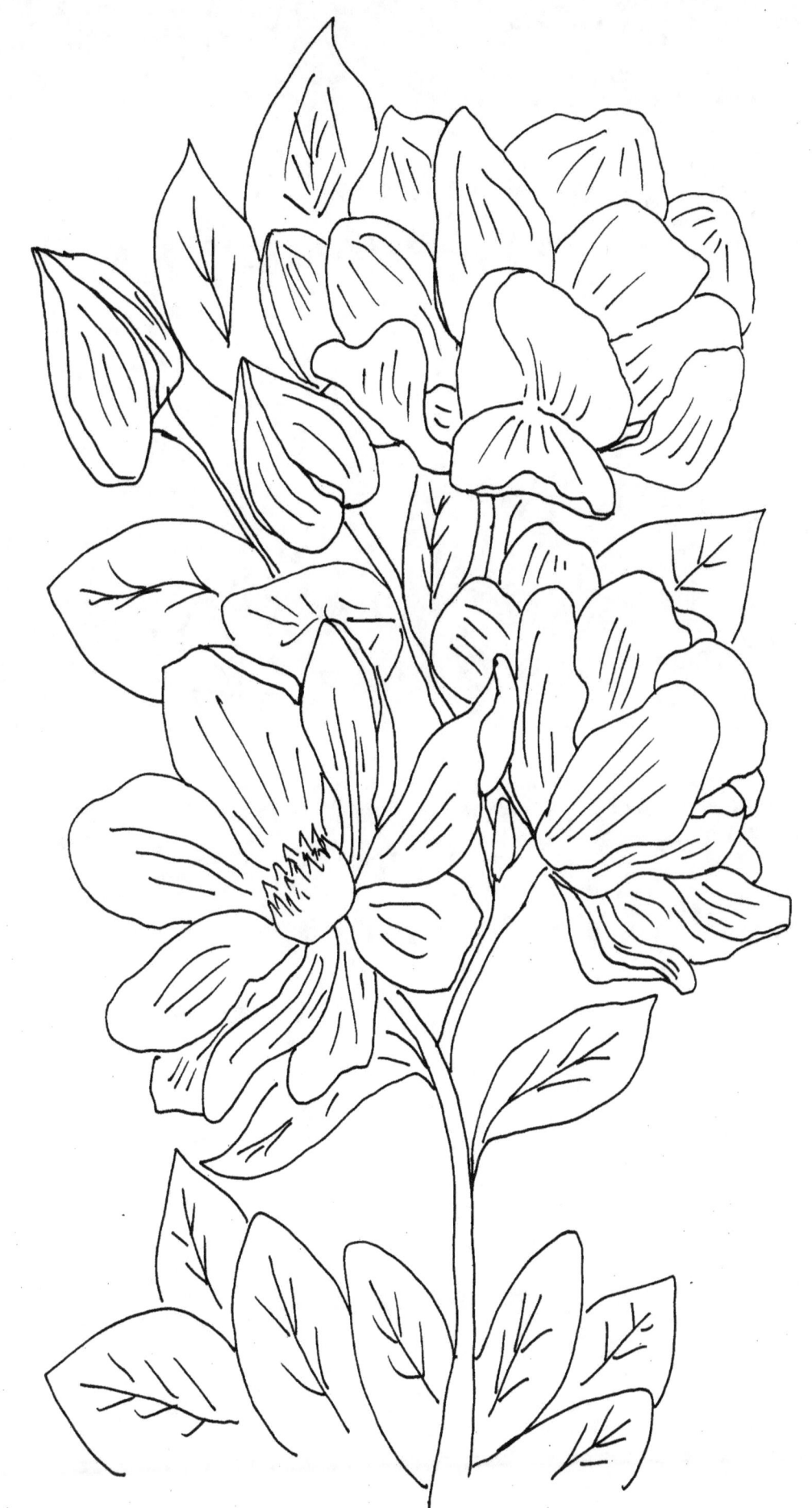

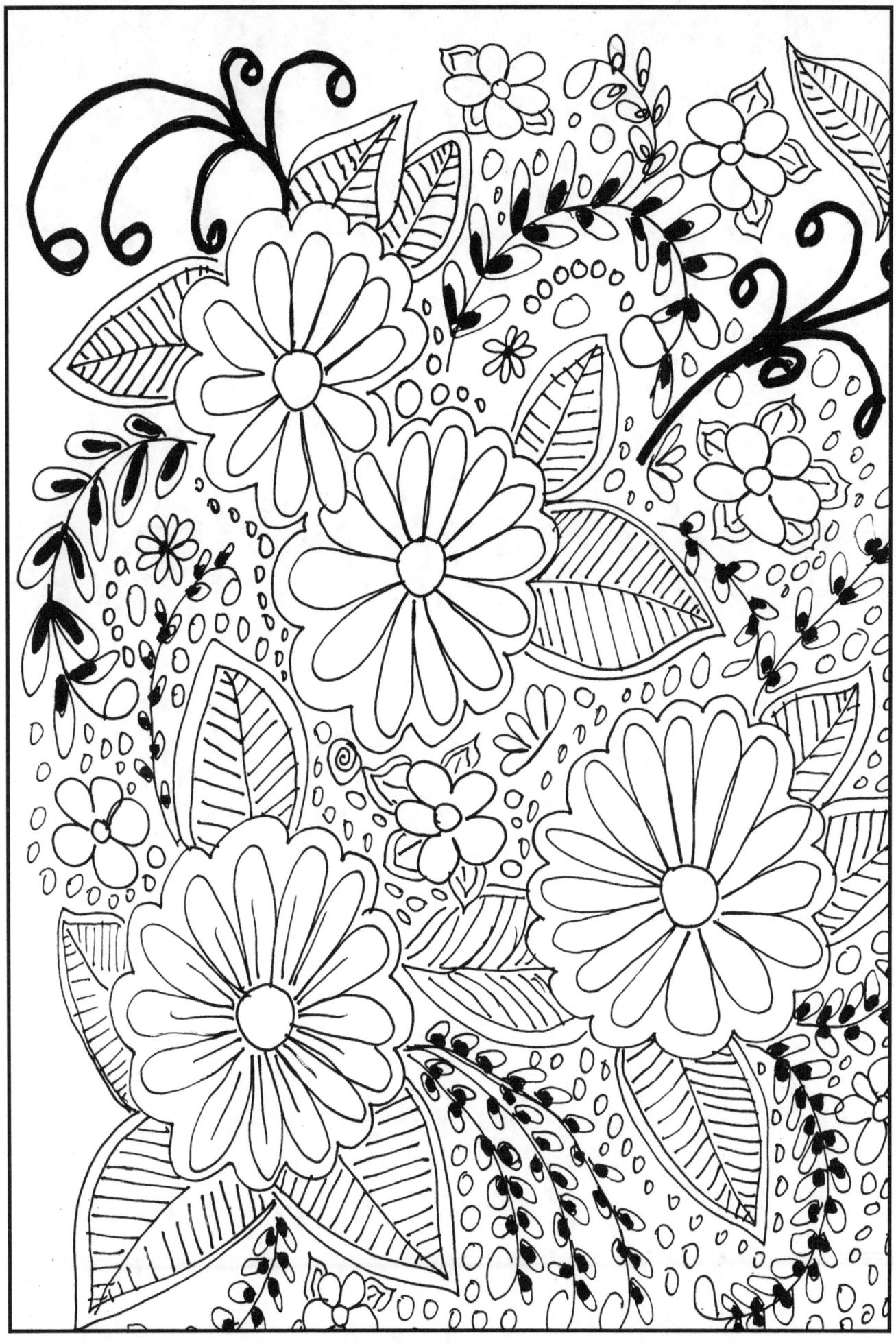

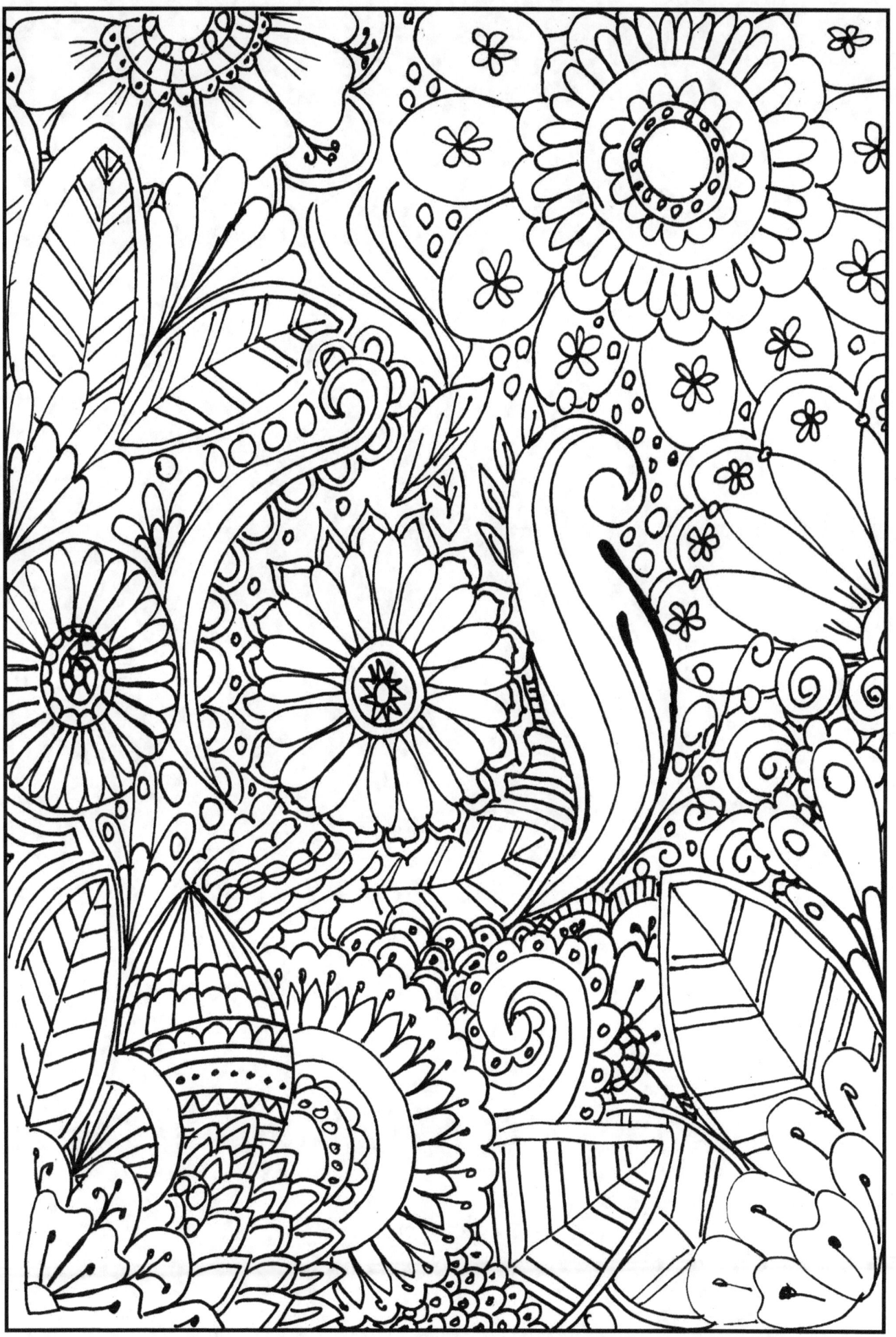

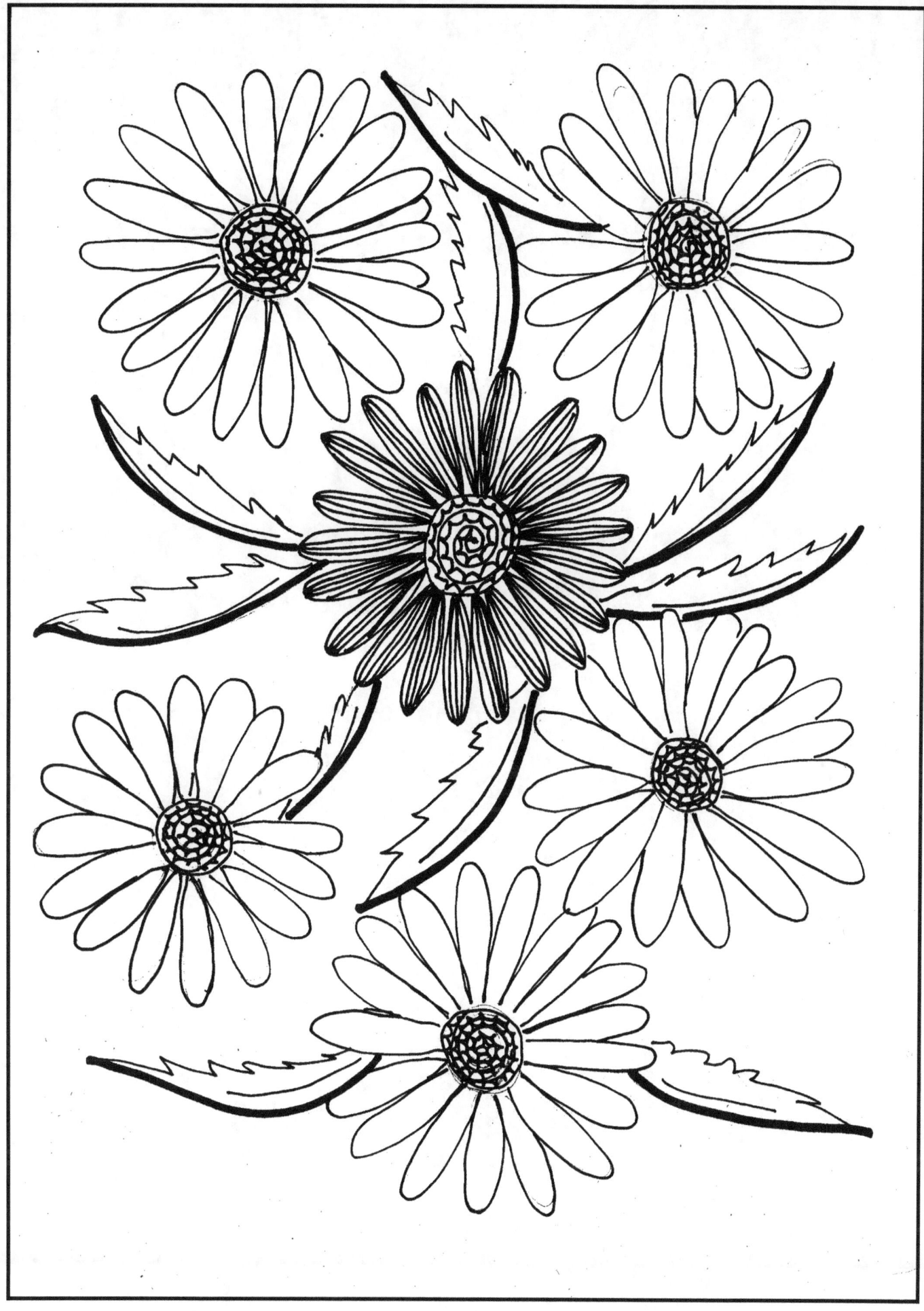

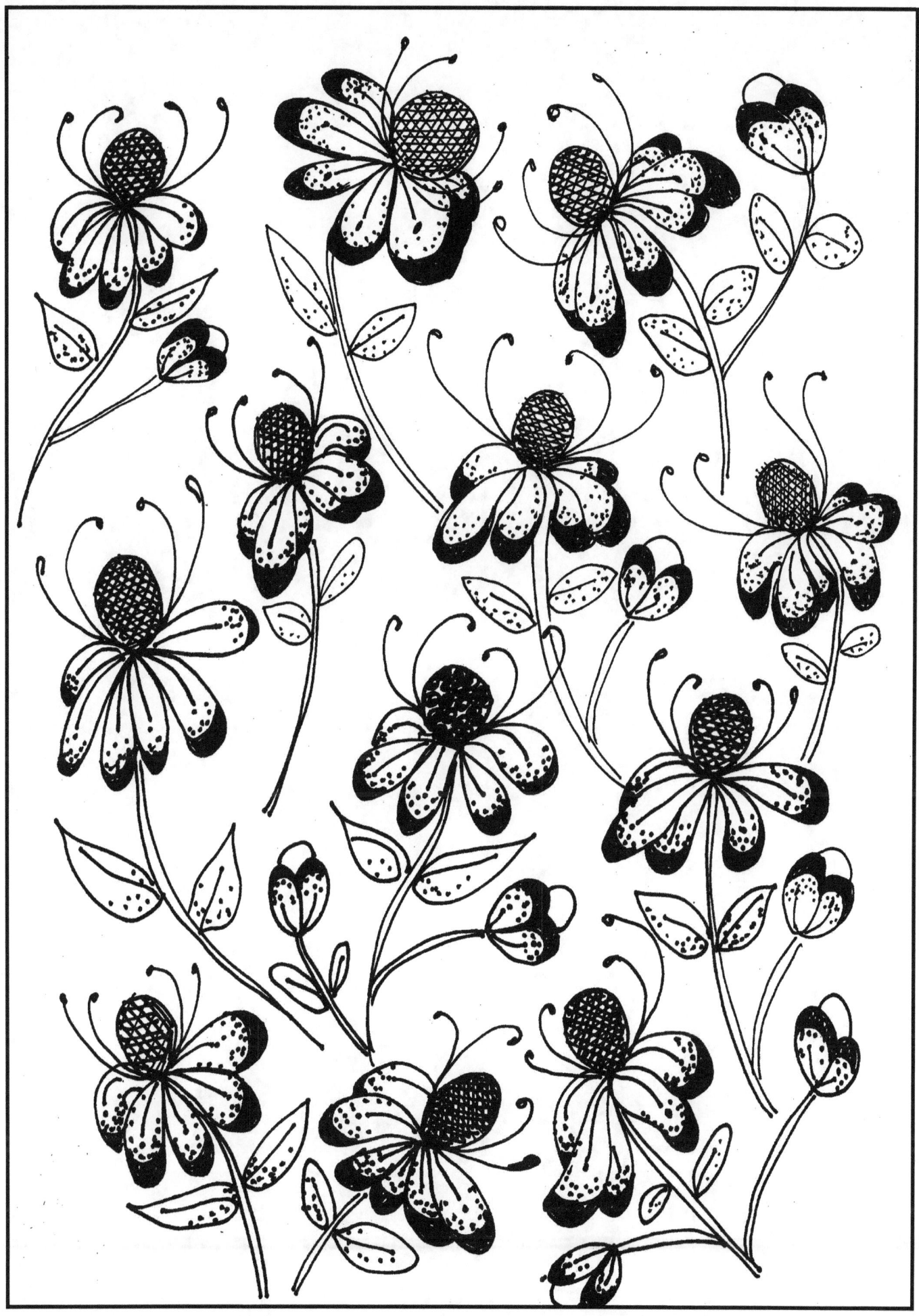

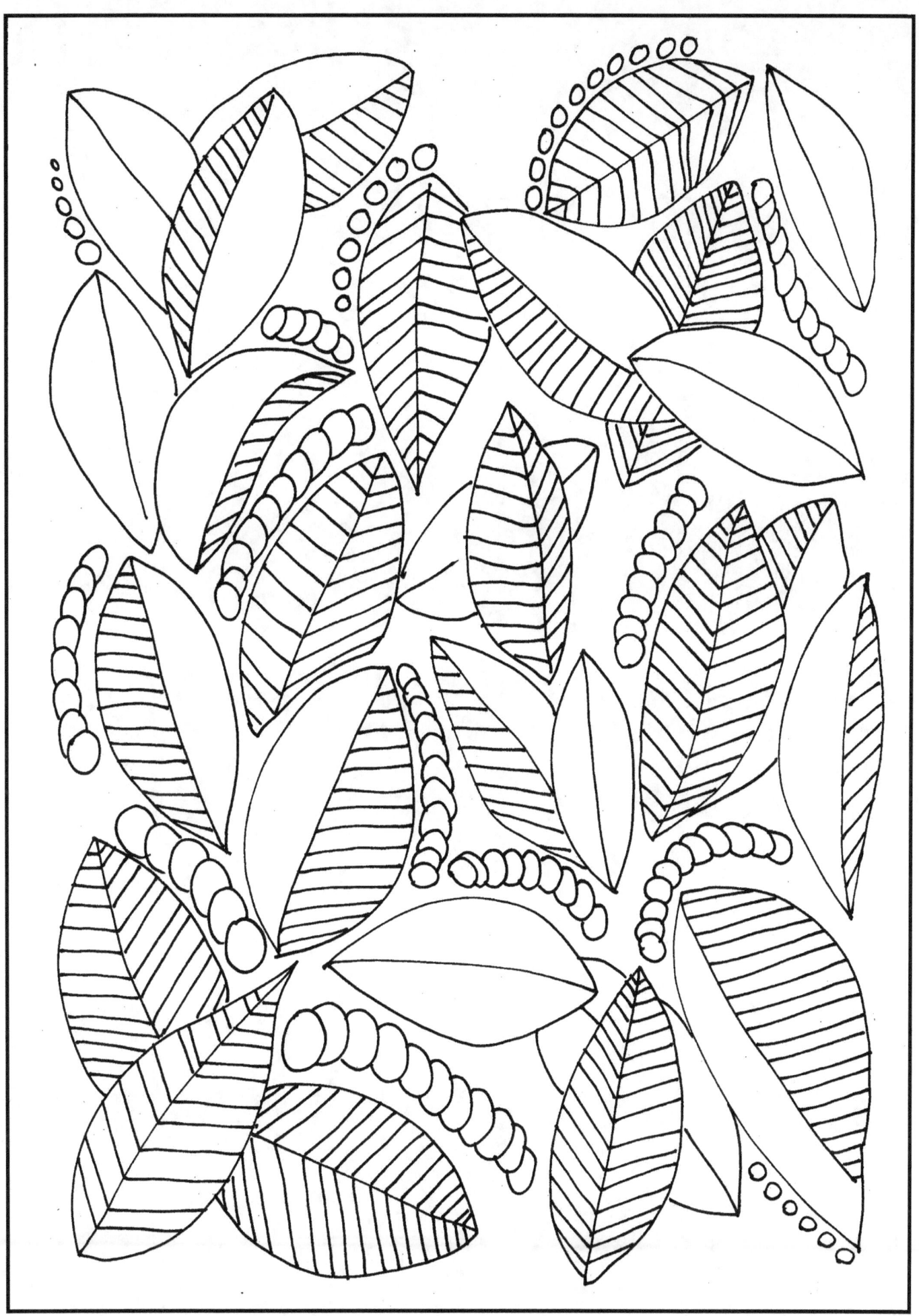

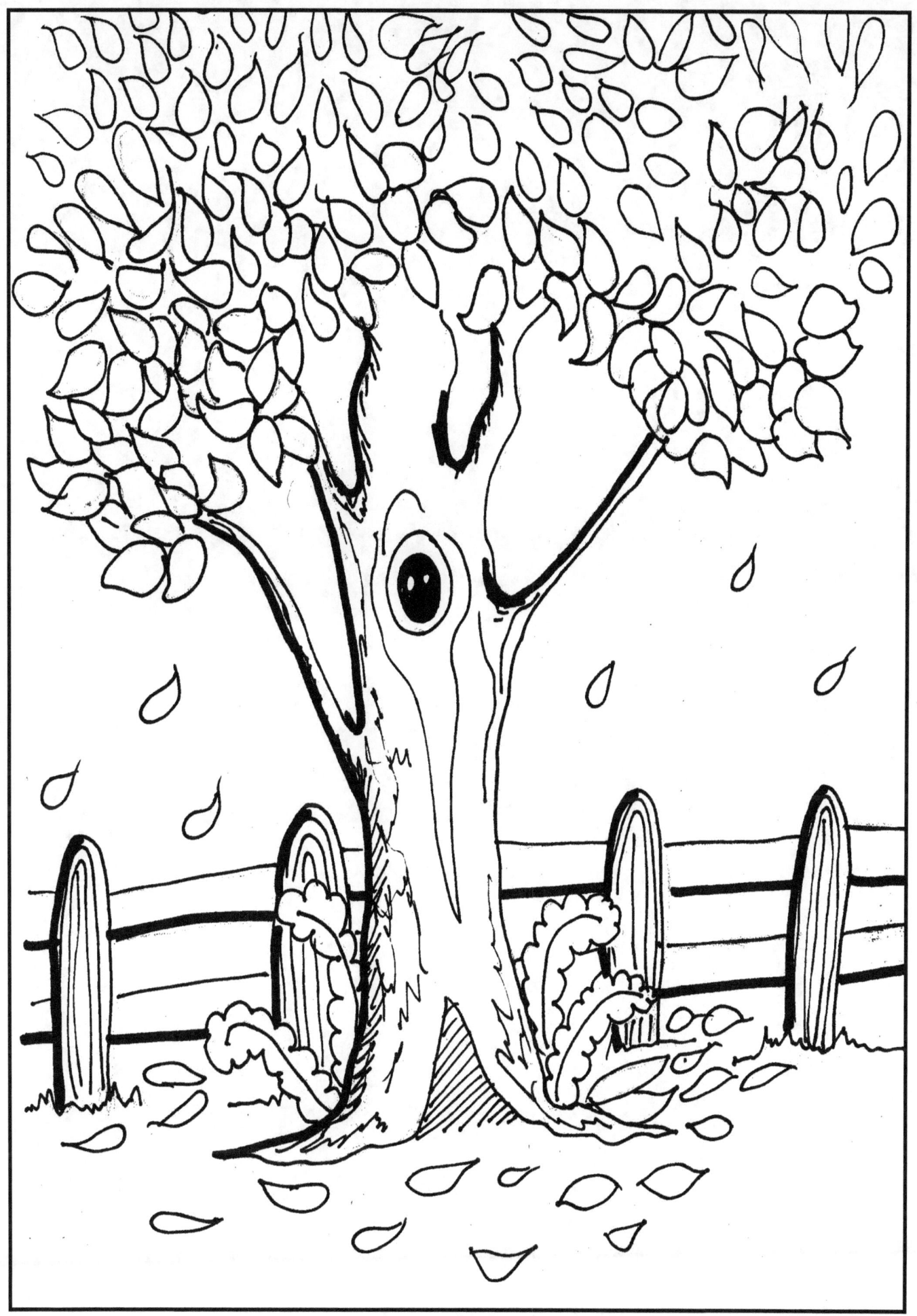

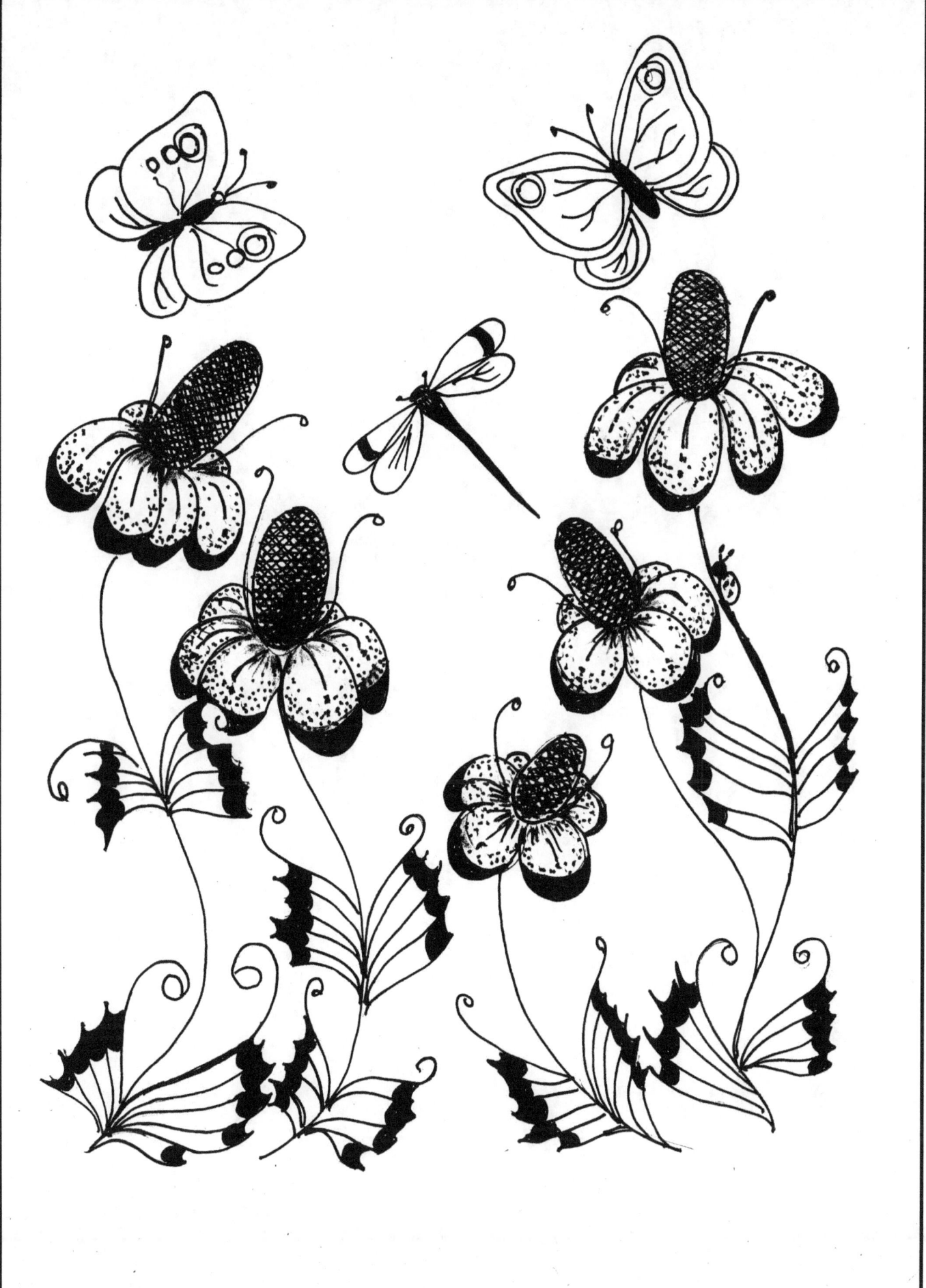

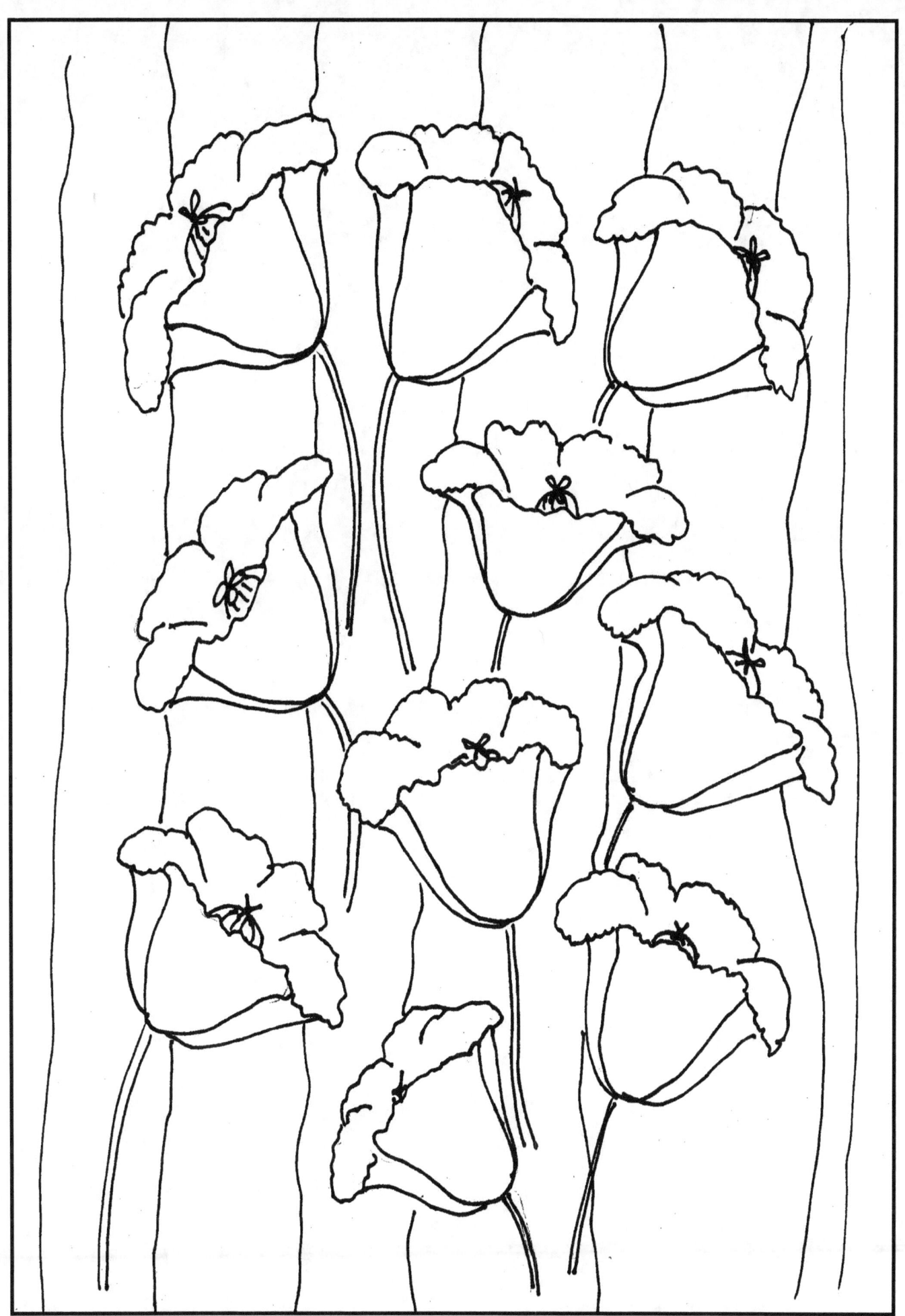

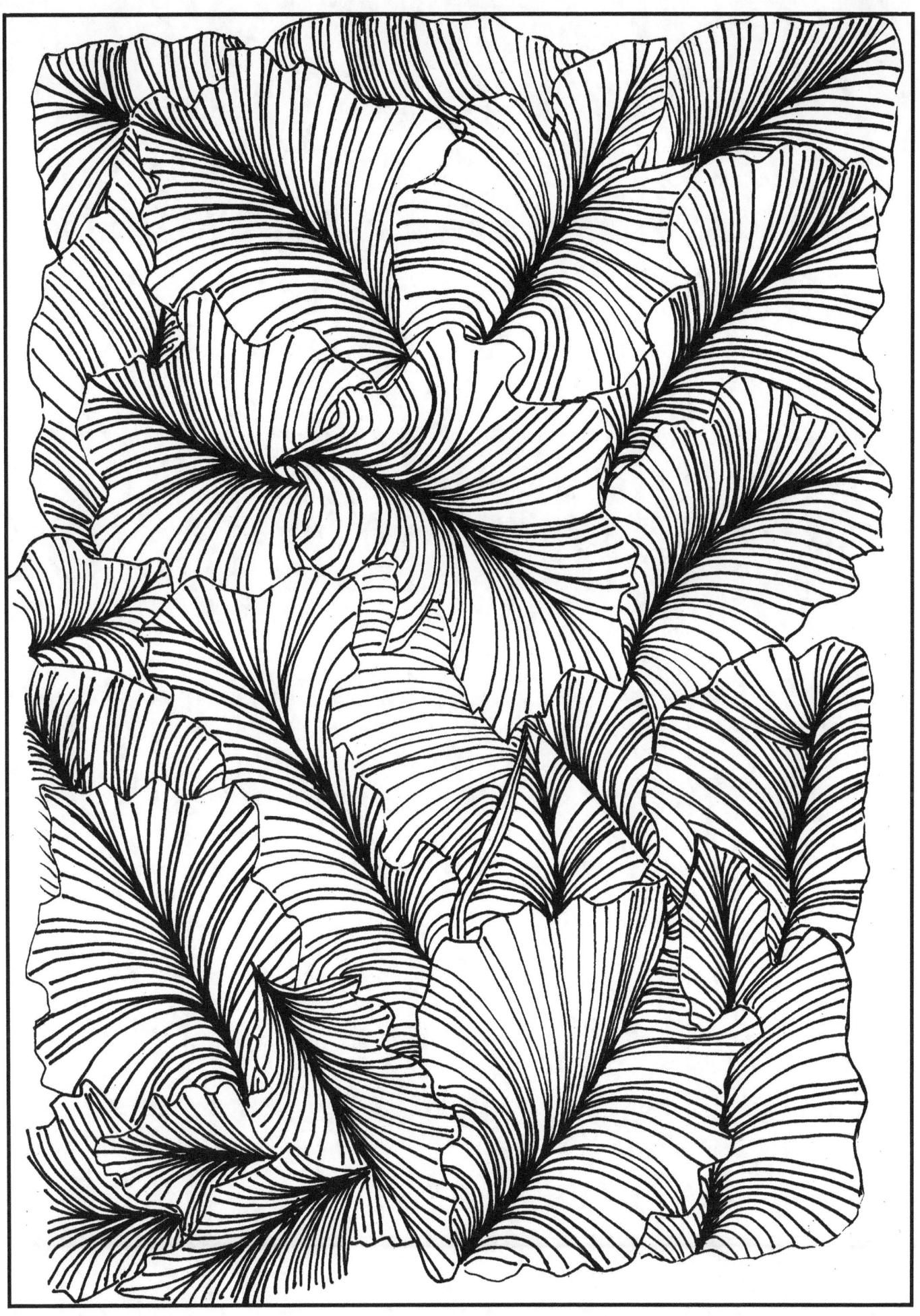

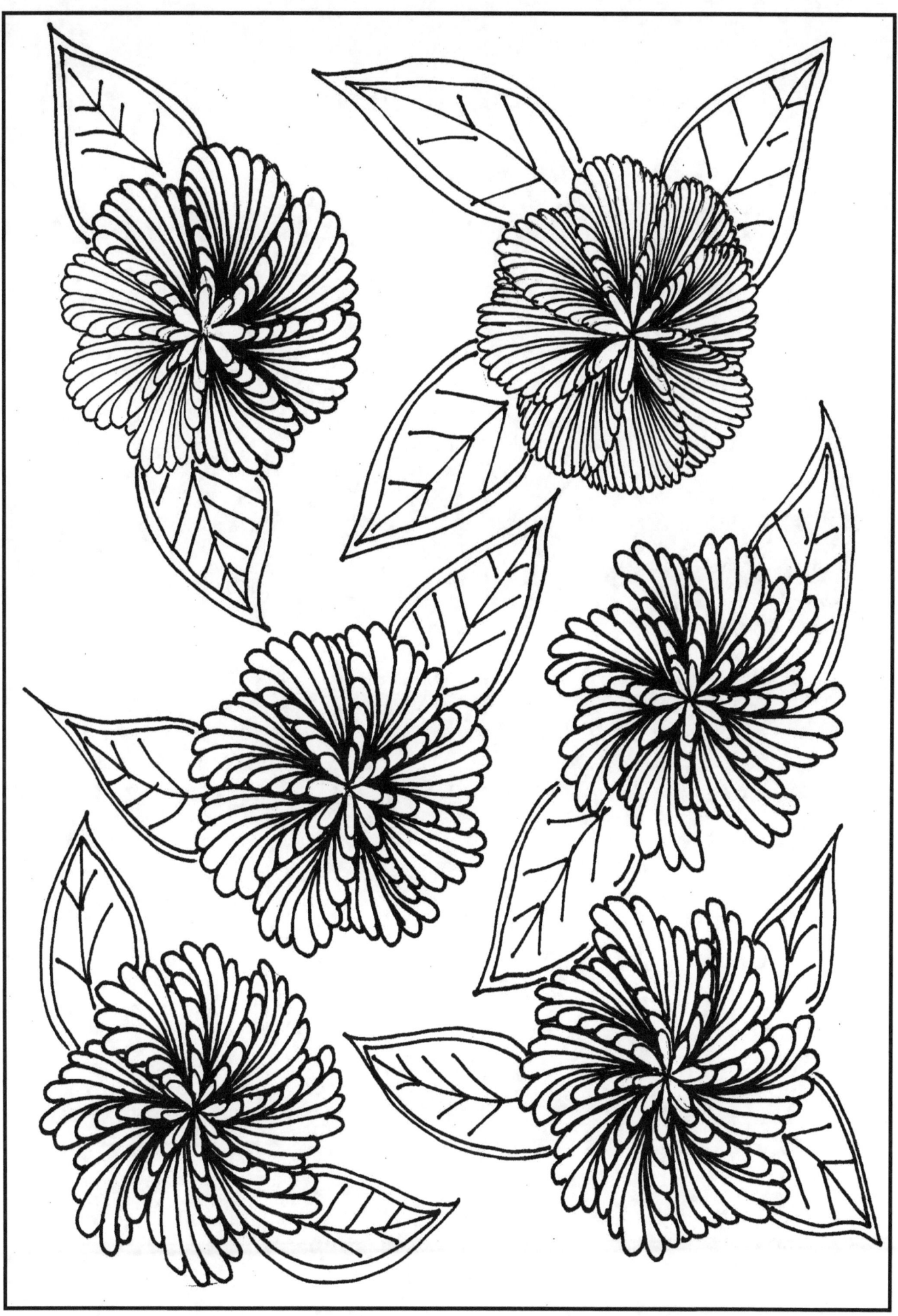

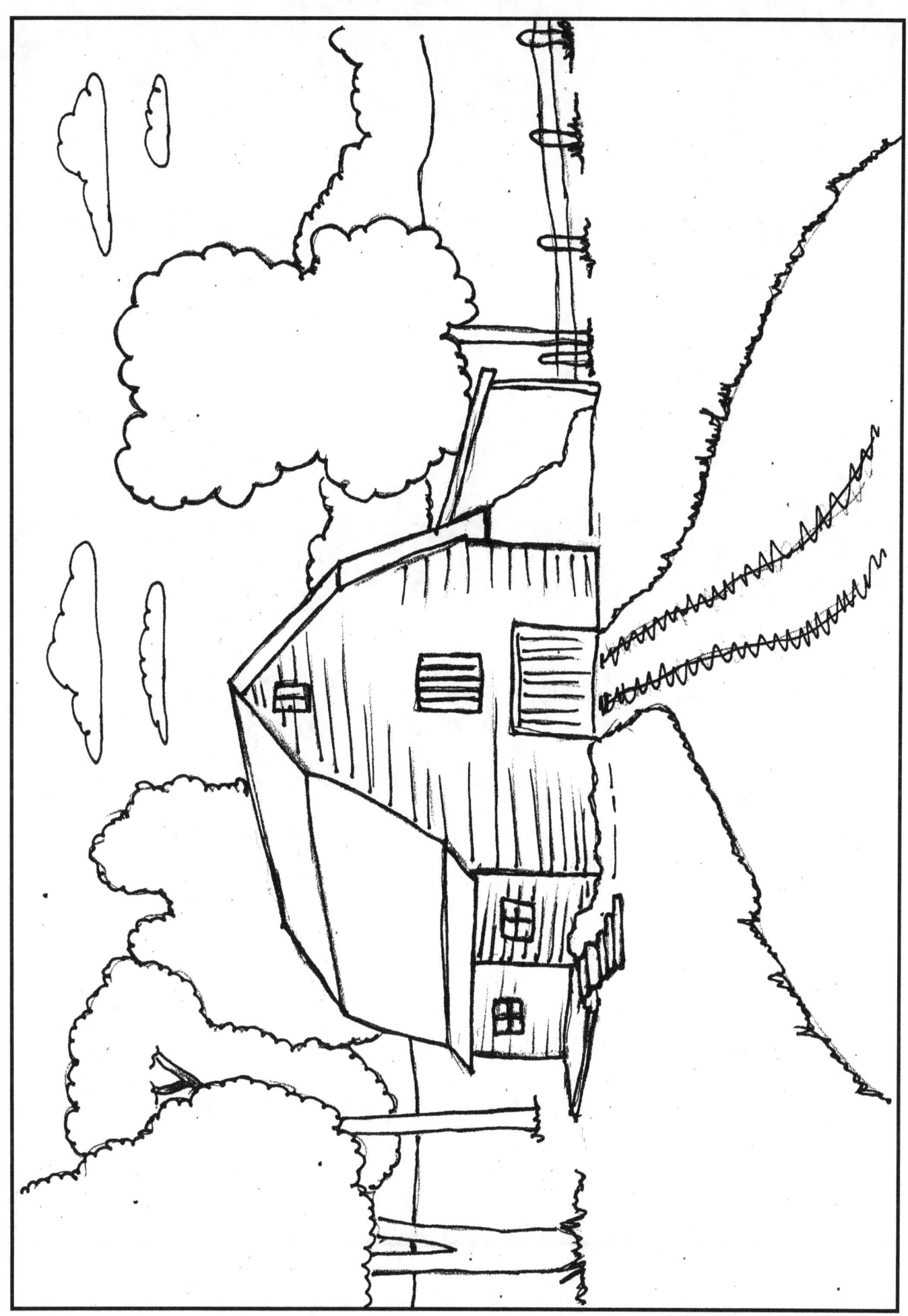

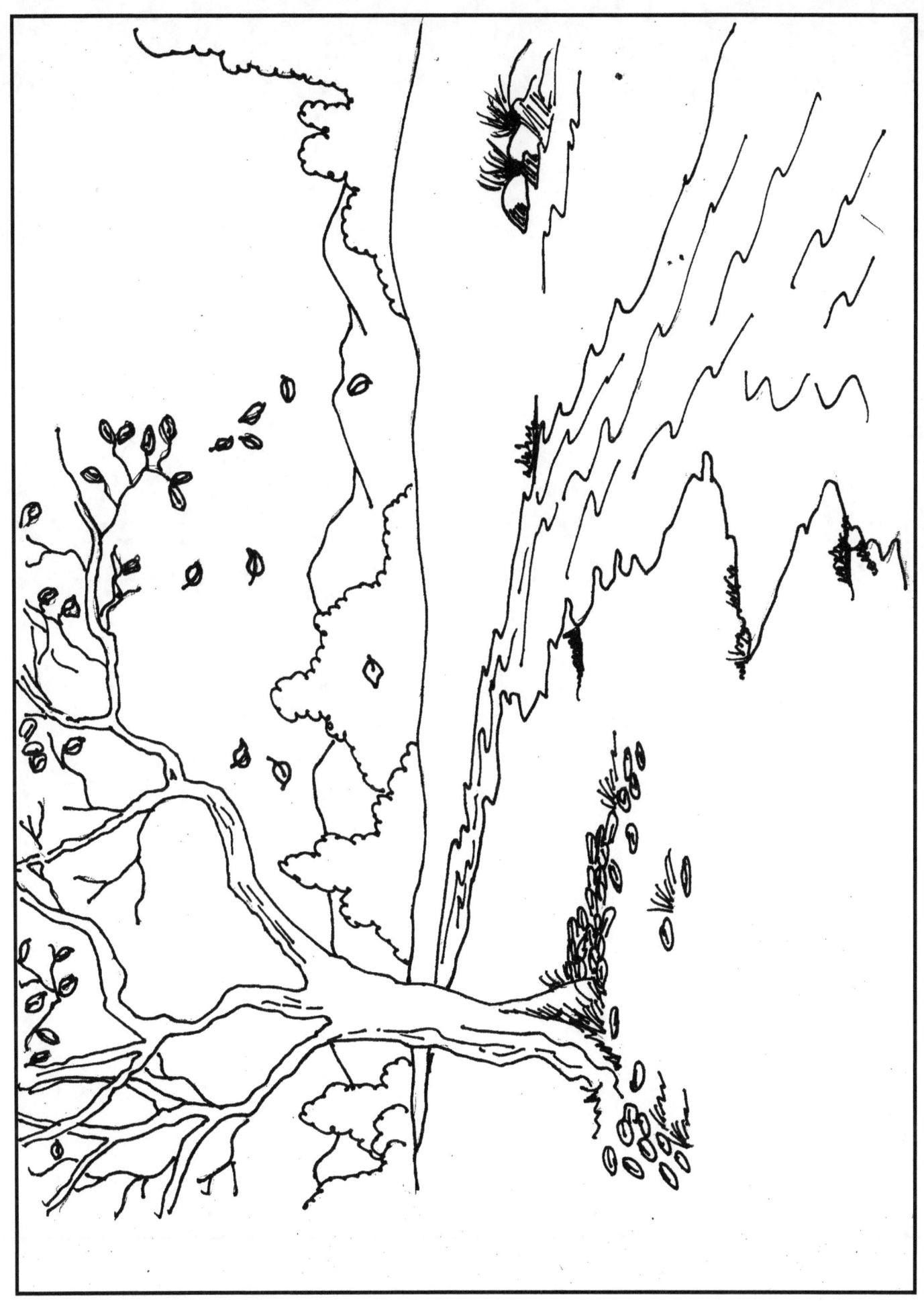

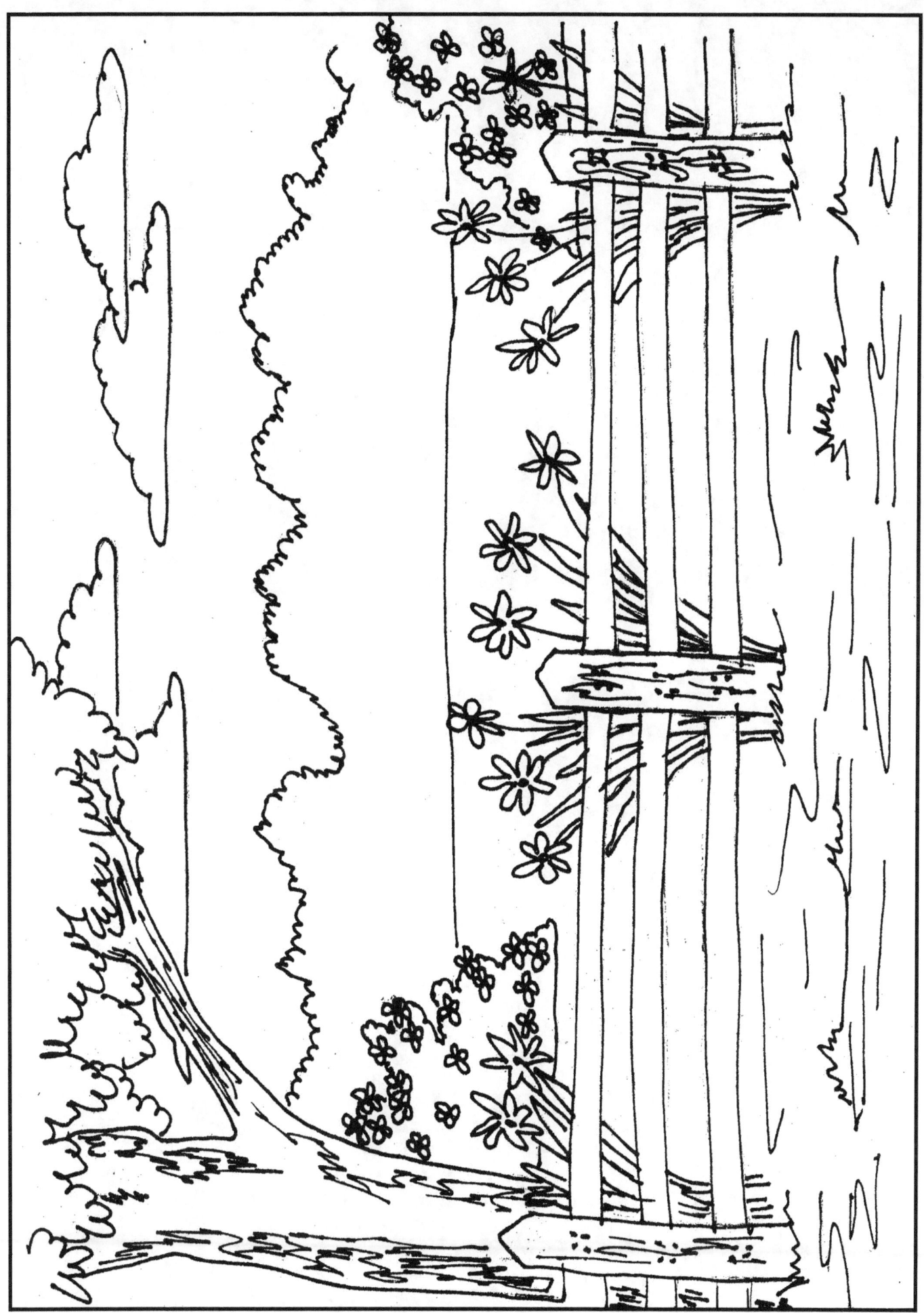

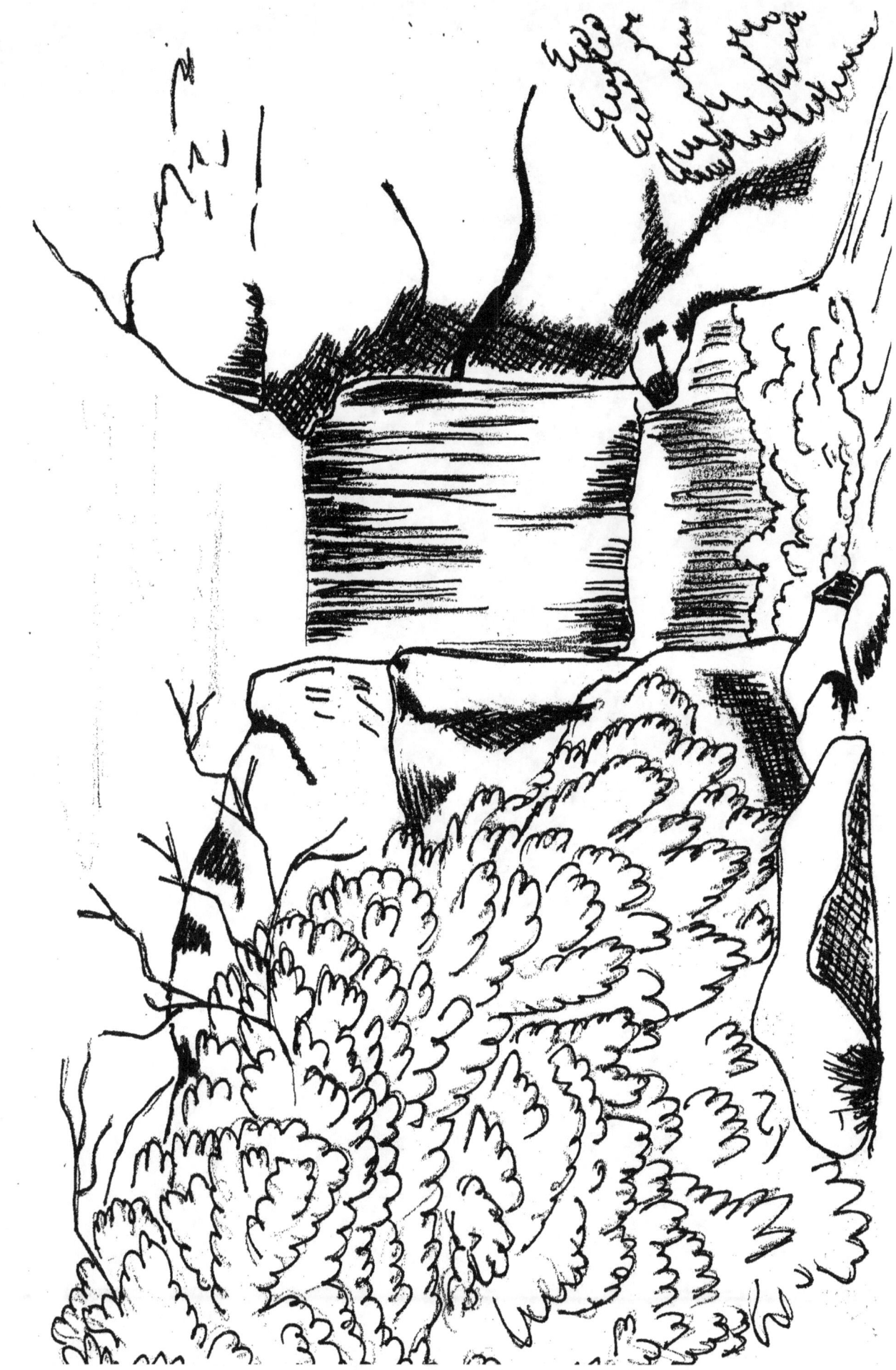

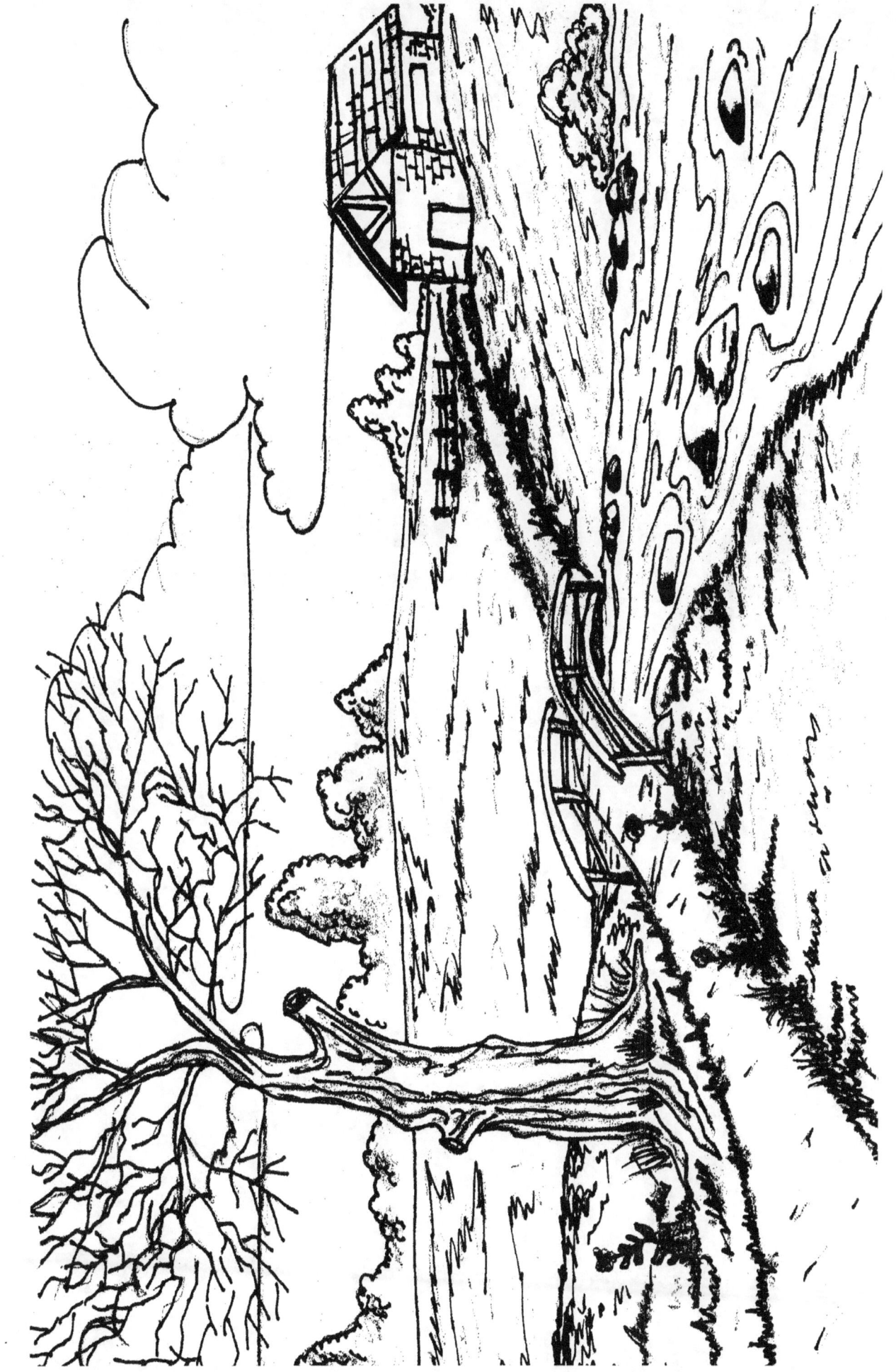

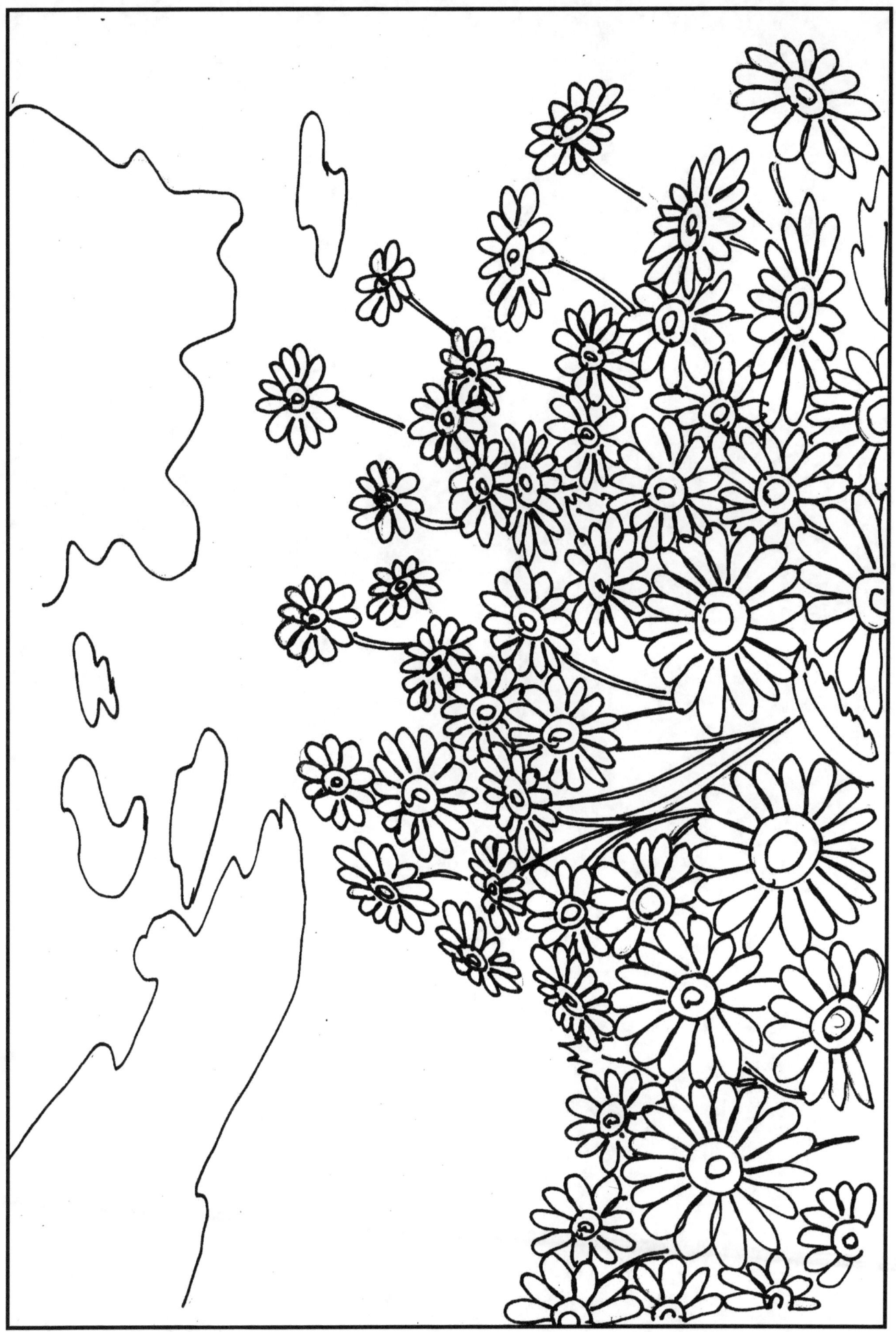

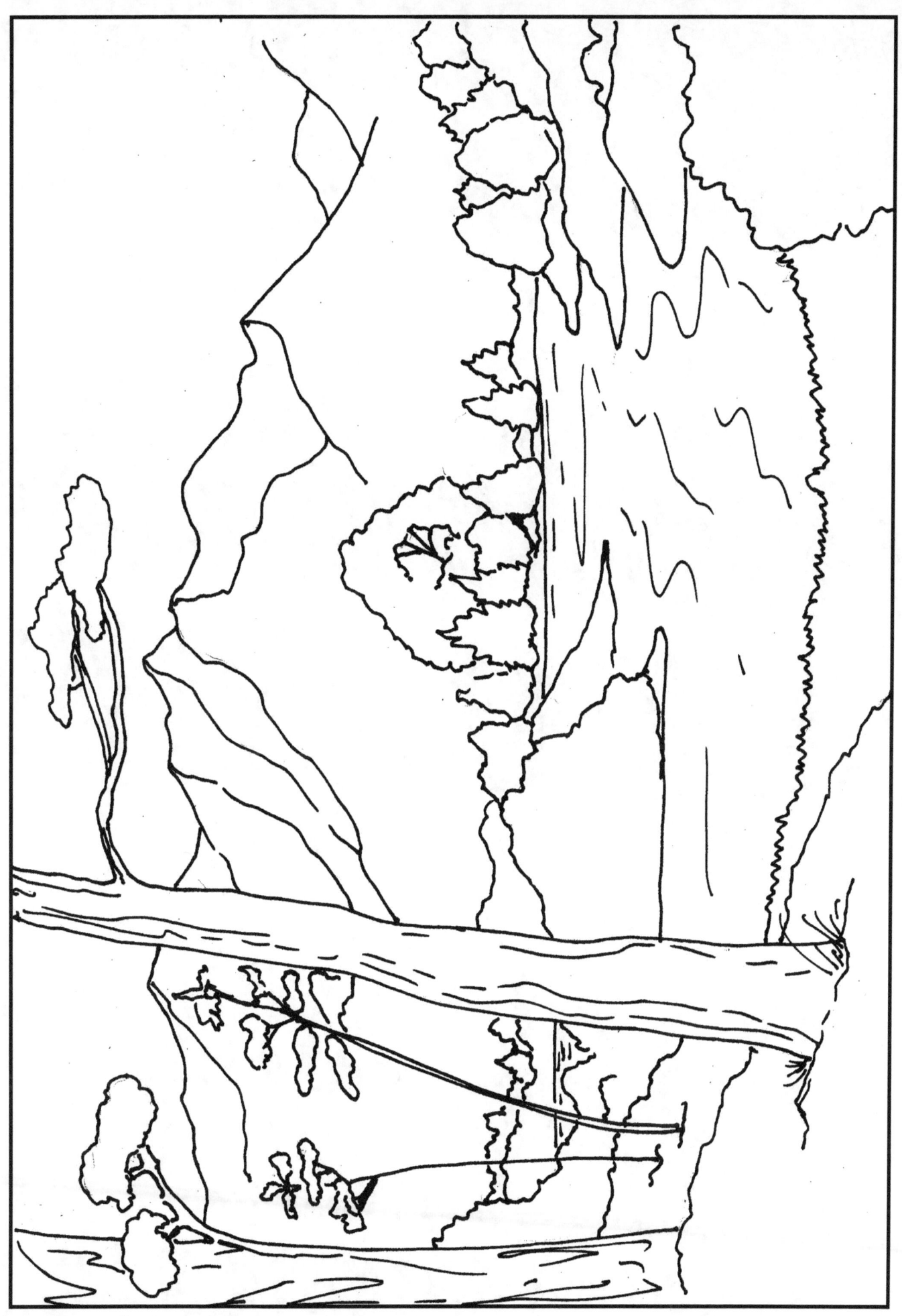

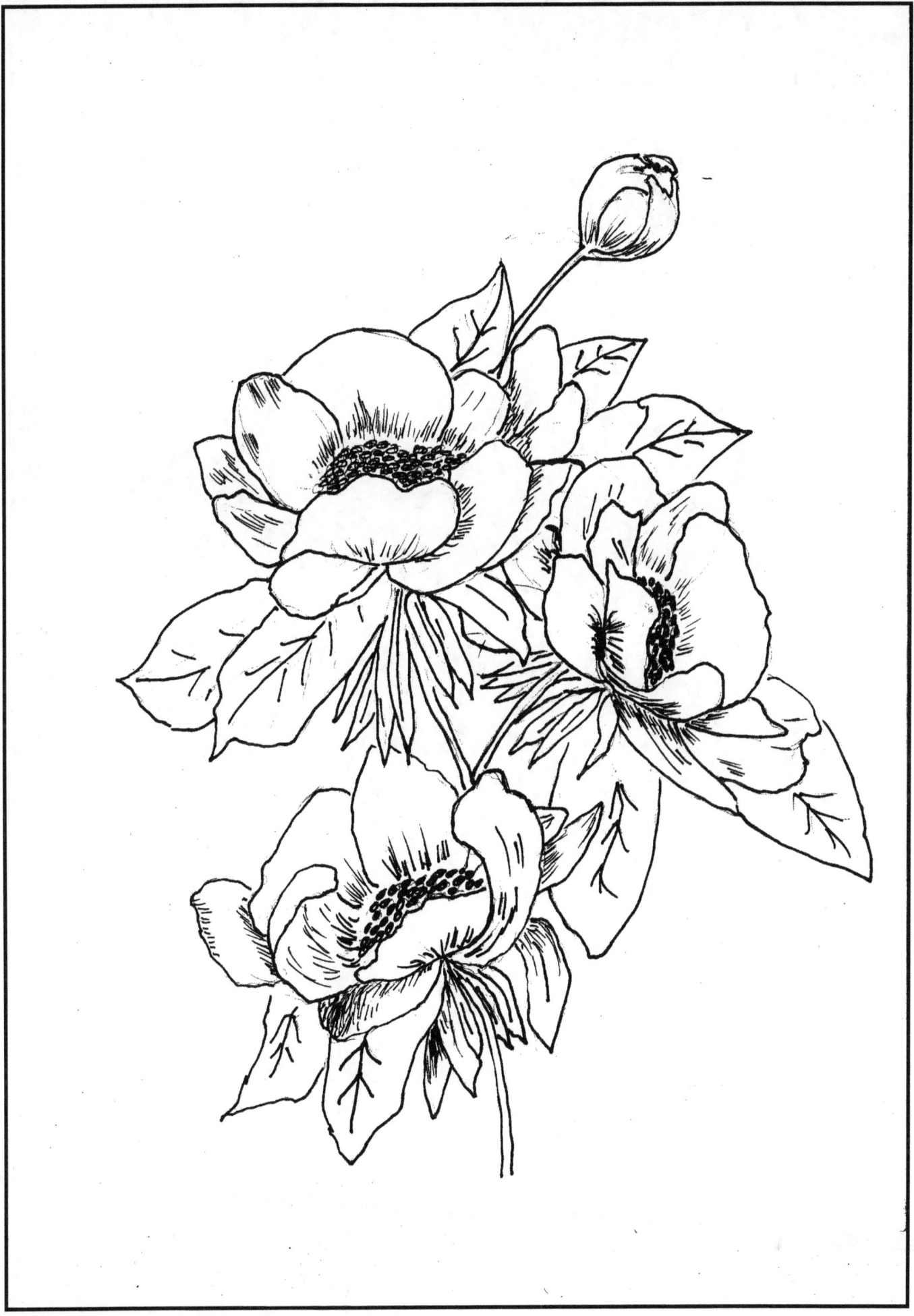

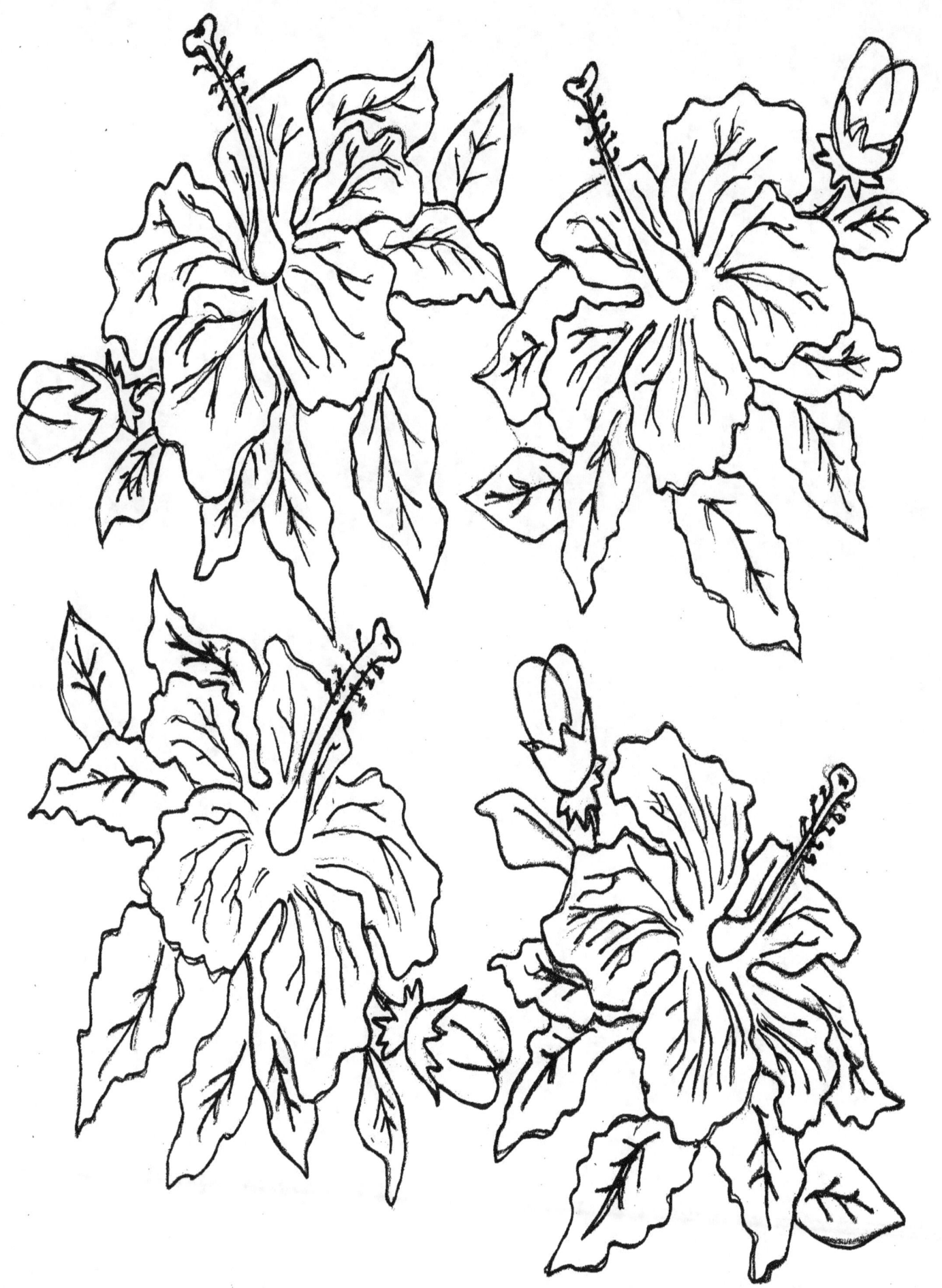

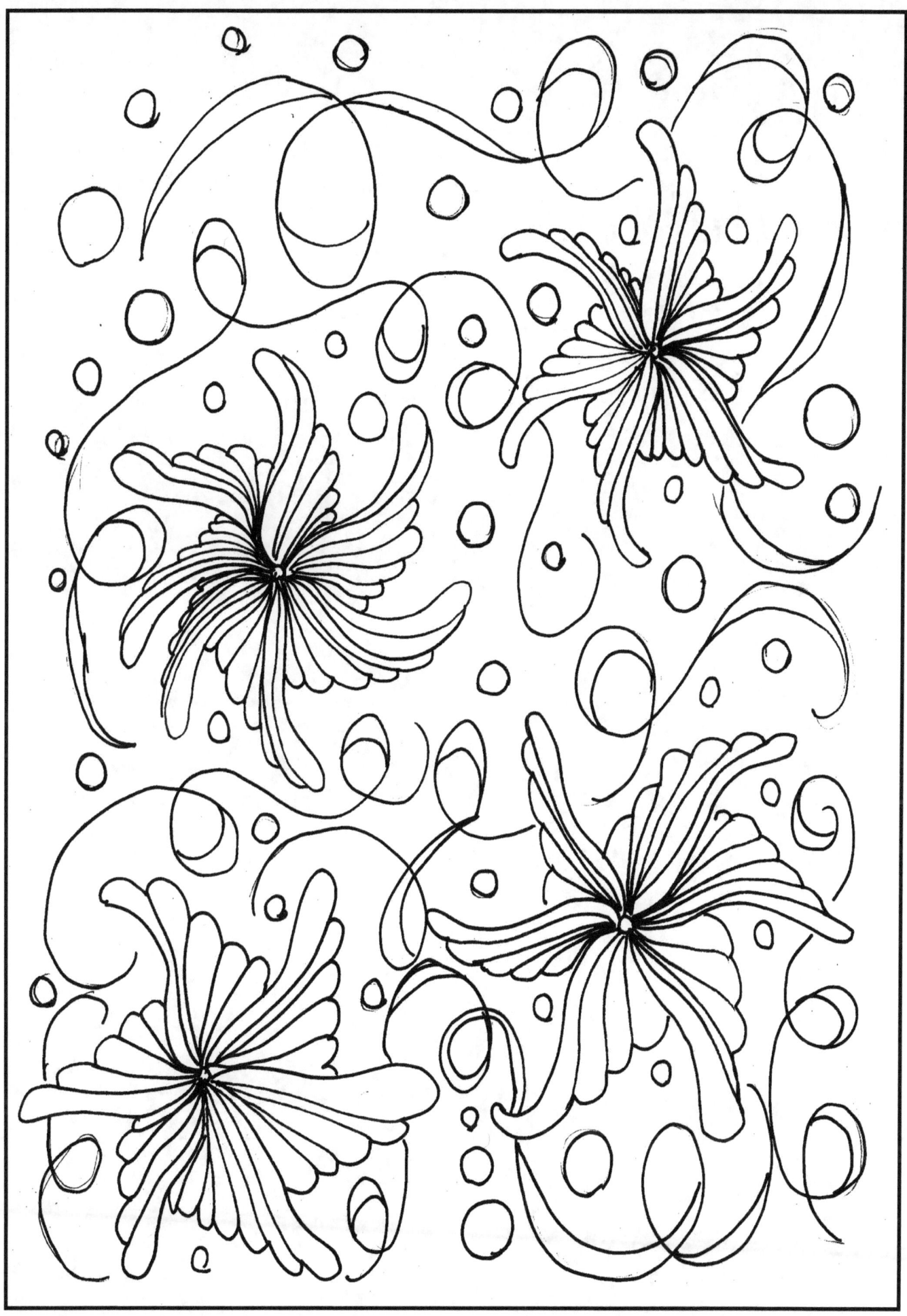

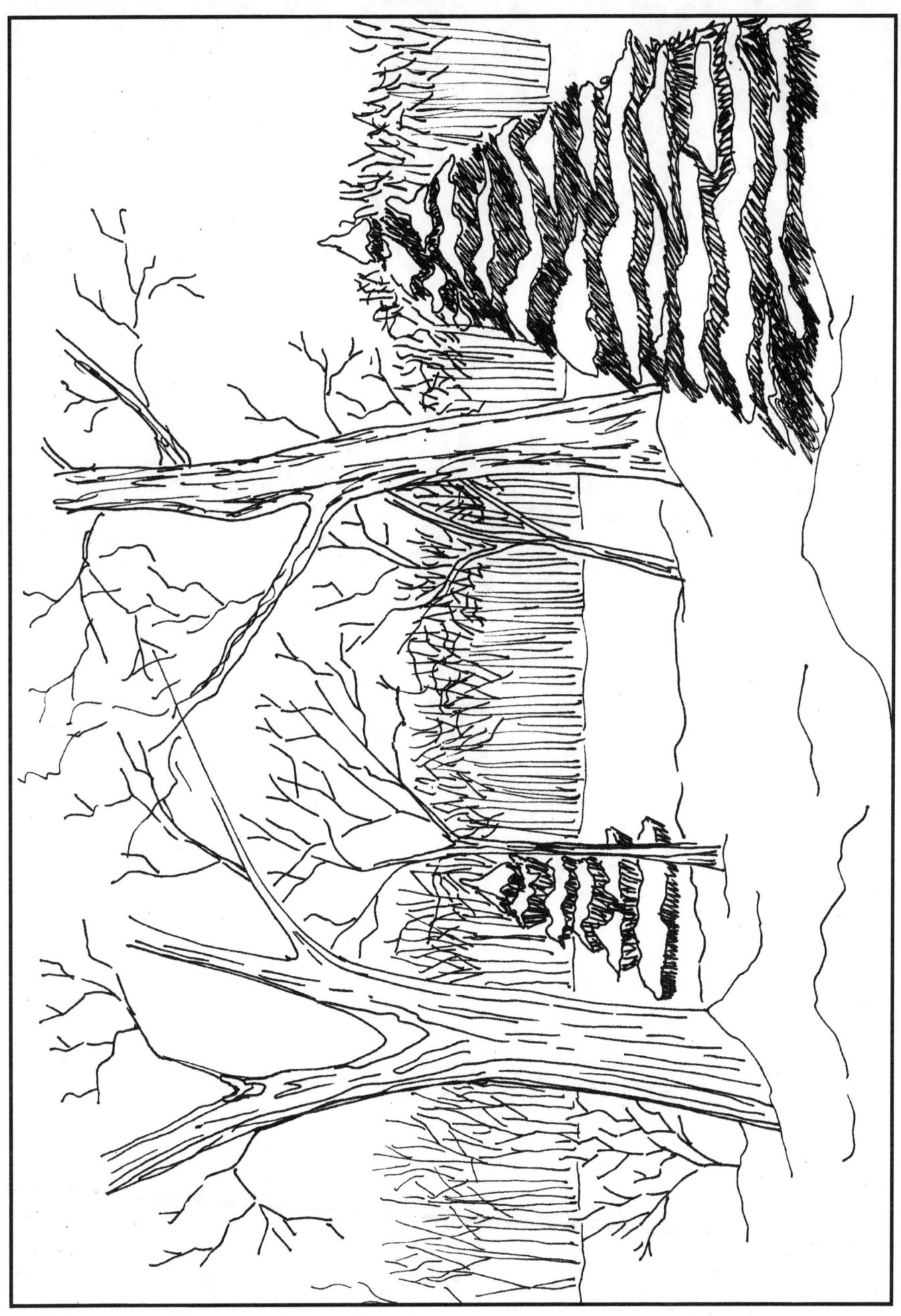

Don't MISS the next issue of The Art of Coloring

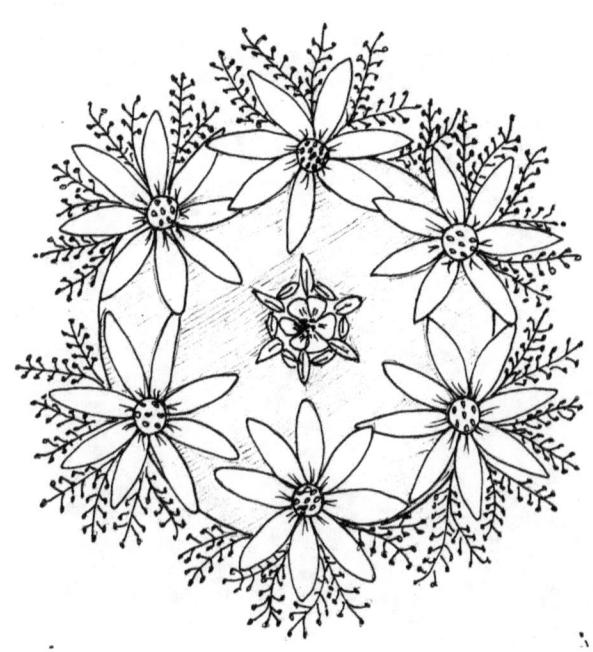

Here is your opportunity to order and review these fabulous books before anyone else does or before they are put out for sale.   Check the books you want and mail with proper funds to:

The Artist Korner

190 County Rd. 41

Heflin, Al 36264

Real Landscapes_____

Landscapes _____

Flower Patterns _____

The Grim Reaper _____

Ole Hippy   _____

Butterflies and Blossoms _____

Great Mandalas _____

Each book is $15.99 includes postage and shipping.

Buy two and get the 3rd one Free

Name: _____

Address:_____

City: _____State: ____Zip:_____

Phone:_____

Email:_____
(optional)

Be sure to include the proper funds. Cash , check or Money order.

Customer Service: (256) 201-7584

Color your STRESS and Anxieties away

I know it works.

I know it works because I have been carrying my art work with me for years. Whenever I go someplace that I must wait like the Doctors office it makes the wait much easier. When asked why I carry my art work to the doctors office, I tell them "That's my Prozac." Being an artist, Illustrator I decided to draw and design my own line of adult coloring books. Try It! When you are stress out and got a lot on your mind , if you are looking for a way to slow down , this is the Ideal way to relieve stress and anxiety.

There is no right or wrong way to color the pages, just start coloring.

The pages are printed on acid free paper and only on one side. Create one of a kind piece of artwork with the medium of your choice.

Thank You for buying our books.
We are positive you will enjoy them.